Biomedical Globalization

Sergio Díaz-Briquets
Charles C. Cheney

Biomedical Globalization

The International Migration of Scientists

Routledge
Taylor & Francis Group

LONDON AND NEW YORK

First published 2002 by Transaction Publishers

Published 2017 by Routledge
2 Park Square, Milton Park, Abingdon, Oxon OX14 4RN
711 Third Avenue, New York, NY 10017, USA

First issued in paperback 2017

Routledge is an imprint of the Taylor & Francis Group, an informa business

Library of Congress Catalog Number: 2002021771

Library of Congress Cataloging-in-Publication Data

Díaz-Briquets, Sergio.
    Biomedical globalization : the international migration of scientists / Sergio Díaz-Briquets and Charles C. Cheney.
        p. cm.
    Includes bibliographical references and index.
    ISBN 0-7658-0104-3 (alk. paper)
    1. Brain drain. 2. Globalization. 3. Emigration and immigration. 4. Scientists—International cooperation. I. Cheney, Charles C. II. Title.
    [DNLM: 1. National Institutes of Health (U.S.) 2. Foreign Professional Personnel—supply and distribution—United States. 3. Research—manpower—United States. 4. Emigration and immigration 5. Research Personnel—organization & administration—United States. W 20.5 D542b 2002]

R852 .D53   2002   2002021771
331.12'791—dc21

ISBN 13: 978-1-138-50767-8 (pbk)
ISBN 13: 978-0-7658-0104-3 (hbk)

To our wives and children

Contents

Acknowledgments

We wish to thank the officials of the National Institutes of Health who opened their doors and provided us with valuable information. Of particular help in facilitating our research were Michael Gottesman, Deputy Director for Intramural Research, Philip S. Chen, Senior Advisor to the Deputy Director for Intramural Research, and James S. Alexander, Deputy Director of the Office of Education. We are also grateful to the many other individuals at the National Institutes of Health and elsewhere who consented to be interviewed and gave generously of their time and thoughts during the course of this study.

Several individuals assisted us in interviewing biomedical constituencies in the United States and abroad. These included Jennifer Ballantine, Janet Corlett, Jorge Casals, Horacio Divito, Jennifer Hirsch, Shuanqing Liu, and Irene Zimmermann de la Torre. The interviews carried out by Elisabeth Herreria in Argentina and Australia were remarkably rich in depth and detail. Our special thanks go to Shelley Howes, who demonstrated exceptional energy, poise, and skill in contacting and interviewing biomedical scientists across the United States and in Europe, in participating with and observing them in a variety of settings and activities, and in analyzing the research findings. Melisa Gamallo was a most helpful research assistant.

Finally, we wish to acknowledge our gratitude to Michael S. Teitelbaum, Program Officer at the Alfred P. Sloan Foundation, for his encouragement when we proposed this study. We would not have been able to pursue this endeavor to a successful conclusion without the generous support extended by the Sloan Foundation to the Council for Human Development.

1

Introduction

There has been much debate in recent years about the impact of the migration to and employment of foreign engineers and computer professionals in the United States. The discussion has generally focused on why these foreign workers are hired, the conditions under which they work, and how their presence in the workforce affects the employment prospects of American workers and the competitiveness of the U.S. economy. However, the presence of foreign biomedical scientists[1] has received less attention. While this may be explained in part by a tighter labor market in the biomedical occupations and the smaller number of persons involved, the fact that employers go to the effort entailed in hiring these foreigners—in a country which enjoys a highly vaunted reputation for excellence in training and producing scientific professionals—merits examination in itself.

The authors undertook this study to shed some light on the factors behind the employment of foreign biomedical scientists in the U.S. labor market by examining several features of the presence of foreign biomedical scientists at the National Institutes of Health (NIH) in Bethesda, Maryland. We selected NIH[2] as the focus of our study because it represents a unique combination of characteristics: It is a federal agency with an academic ambiance that conducts biomedical research and training internally while supporting these activities externally through grants and contracts with a host of academic institutions and biotechnology companies. In our study, postdoctoral ("postdoc") trainees were of key interest, but attention was also devoted to other training and employment categories in which foreign biomedical scientists find their way to NIH. The importance of the foreign postdoc population at NIH is considerable because it accounts for 6 to 7 percent[3] of all biomedical postdocs present during any given year at American training institutions. Our intent was to assess how their presence at this federal research institution is linked to their broader labor market participation. By focusing on NIH and the foreign biomedical scientists that are found there, the study sought to provide a different perspective from that of other related studies that have examined the employment of foreign engineers and computer professionals in universities and the private sector.

The study had several objectives. It was designed to gain an appreciation of (1) why foreign nonimmigrant and immigrant scientists instead of U.S. scientists occupy temporary training and research slots at NIH; (2) how foreign and American scientists at NIH compare in training, skills, motivations, and backgrounds, as well as in terms of working conditions and compensation; (3) the impact that the recruiting of foreign scientists may have on the employment prospects and conditions of their American counterparts; (4) the implications that these hiring and employment trends may hold for American training institutions and scientific expertise; and (5) the implications of the foreign scientists' presence for U.S. immigration and labor policies.

Related research questions revolved around the eventual commercial impact of the presence of foreign scientists at NIH (whether to the benefit or detriment of the American economy); benefits that accrue to NIH by recruiting the highly trained, regardless of nationality; and how the foreign-scientist pool at NIH contributes to the development of the American biotechnology industry, especially in the neighboring Bethesda area of Maryland. The study gave some attention to the relationship between NIH and the university teaching and research community, as well as to the mechanisms whereby foreign biomedical scientific trainees join the U.S. labor force, whether in a temporary or permanent capacity.

We carried out the bulk of our field research in the NIH community between June of 1997 and July of 1999. Extensive individual and small-group interviews captured the experiences and perceptions of a range of persons engaged in biomedical research and training regarding the presence of significant numbers of foreign scientists at NIH and in American educational institutions and biotechnology firms. To ensure candor, those interviewed were assured confidentiality, except for a few NIH senior officials who spoke on behalf of the institution for the record. Follow-up contacts were sometimes made to clarify points and to augment information gained during initial interviews.

In addition to talking with individuals on the NIH campus and in the surrounding area, the research team participated with and observed them in a spectrum of other settings and activities. These encompassed NIH-sponsored conferences and job fairs, as well as social and career-oriented events organized by NIH-based entities that bring together scientists who share a common cultural heritage (such as Chinese) or come from regional groups of countries (such as the European Union). Further, we took part in international biomedical association conference activities and talked with representatives of American and foreign educational institutions and biotechnology firms.

We began this process by contacting biomedical scientists at NIH and in other locations who were previously known to us, and we then conducted open-ended interviews with them according to a written guide designed for that purpose. Also, many persons were identified and interviewed at conferences and other scientific and social functions attended by members of the research team. For example, in the summer of 1997, three research team members took part in a traditional Chinese banquet as guests of NIH's Chinese Scholars Association to celebrate Great Britain's return of Hong Kong to the People's Republic of China. This association represents all persons of Chinese heritage at NIH regardless of political or national affiliation, and therefore it afforded the researchers a valuable mechanism for meeting and interacting with many members of NIH's large Chinese community.

Once we had met individuals and interviewed them, they referred us to others within their social and professional networks. This "snowballing" procedure continued until it was determined that a representative range of persons within a number of categories had been interviewed, and until it became evident that interviewing had ceased to yield new insights relevant to the study. Over the course of two years, the researchers held in-depth interviews with approximately 200 persons, and they interacted conversationally with about 300 in total.

The interviewed individuals belonged to the following informant categories:

- current NIH administrators and scientists
- former NIH administrators and scientists
- current NIH American trainees
- former NIH American trainees

- current NIH foreign trainees
- former NIH foreign trainees abroad
- former NIH foreign trainees in the United States
- U.S. educational institution faculty
- U.S. educational institution American trainees
- U.S. educational institution foreign trainees
- U.S. biotechnology firm representatives and scientists
- Representatives of U.S. professional biomedical associations and commercial biotechnology commercial association representatives
- immigration attorneys

These thirteen categories were not mutually exclusive in membership. In fact, many former NIH administrators and scientists, as well as former NIH American and foreign trainees, were found in U.S. educational institutions, biotechnology firms, and professional and commercial associations.

The current and former NIH administrators and scientists included individuals in a number of intramural leadership posts, including the Deputy Director for Intramural Affairs, who granted the investigators an interview, as well as persons representative of NIH's many institutes and centers, who ranged from institute scientific directors to laboratory assistants. The NIH trainees, both American and foreign, were found in a cross-section of NIH's institutes and centers, and those from abroad came from many homelands. It was more difficult to contact and interview former NIH foreign trainees who had left the United States, but a measure of success was achieved nonetheless. This was especially the case regarding scientists who had relocated in Argentina, Australia, and Europe.

In the interviews conducted during the course of field research, persons in all categories were asked to offer their views on certain common themes and various subtopics. These were as follows:

- Reasons for the presence of significant numbers of foreign biomedical scientists and trainees at NIH, American educational institutions, and American biotechnology firms (e.g., types of training, specific disciplines or specialties; certain skills, motivation, performance; relative cost; to forge international connections, promote cross-national research);
- Comparisons of foreign and American biomedical scientists and trainees at NIH, American educational institutions, and American biotechnology firms (e.g., disciplines and specialty areas; skills, motivation,

performance; cultural differences; functions performed; conditions of work; compensation);

- Implications of the presence of foreign biomedical scientists and trainees for the employment of American scientists and trainees (e.g., competition; job prospects and conditions);
- Implications of the presence of foreign biomedical scientists and trainees for American educational institutions and national expertise in science;
- Implications of the presence of foreign biomedical scientists and trainees for American international competitiveness in biomedical research and biotechnological (research and development) applications;
- Implications of the presence of foreign biomedical scientists and trainees for American immigration and labor policies.

Similarities and differences in the experiences and perspectives of the various categories of stakeholders were revealed in their discussions of these central themes.

The overall context for the study is provided in the next chapter. We begin by considering how globalization is related to the international mobility of highly skilled labor. This is followed by a brief description of major recent trends in biomedical research, including the emergence of the biotechnology industry. The discussion includes an overview of the growing debate regarding the training and labor market prospects of American biomedical scientists, including how they are affected by the immigration of foreign scientists to the United States.

Core findings of the study are presented in chapter 3. The chapter begins with an overview of NIH, and the remainder is devoted to the varying perspectives and experiences of different types of current and former NIH personnel who were interviewed during the course of the study. These are organized by principal areas of inquiry and presented according to category of NIH interviewees.

Chapter 4 considers perspectives from outside NIH, including those of academic biomedical faculty and graduate students, biotechnology industry representatives, and spokespersons for biomedical and biotechnology associations. In chapter 5, the immigration process is addressed, and specific attention is given to procedures whereby foreign scientists adjust their visa status to remain in the United States, whether on temporary or permanent bases. This discussion draws heavily on interviews with and written materials provided by immigration attorneys. The study's conclusions are presented in chapter 6.

This study has five appendices. The first describes research opportunities, including conditions of appointment, for foreign scientists at NIH, and the second reviews the various programs of NIH's Fogarty International Center. The third appendix identifies and describes the most commonly used types of visas granted to foreign scientists for either training or working at NIH. The fourth one provides trend data on the number of foreign scientists at NIH by country of origin. And the final appendix presents the new nomenclature NIH began to utilize in 1999 to describe the various categories of research and training appointments available to U.S. and foreign scientists.

Notes

1. In this study, the term life scientist is occasionally used interchangeably with the term biomedical scientist, but of course the two are not identical. The former is broader and includes the work of biological scientists not involved in health-related research. However, since all life processes have a common foundation and some of the sources consulted and cited in this study use the more inclusive definition, when appropriate we, too, use the term life science to accurately represent the sources consulted.
2. It is the custom of those associated with NIH to preface the abbreviation with a definite article—thus, "the NIH." However, in the report we have followed the more common practice of not prefacing the abbreviation.
3. The National Research Council (1998:28) estimated that in 1998 there were 20,000 life science postdocs although the number could well be higher. In 1996, according to unpublished figures, the number of foreign scientists at NIH reached 2,295. The majority of the foreign scientists were postdocs.

2

The Context

Globalization and International Migration

In the new global context, as noted by Ellis (1994) in his discussion of the challenges confronting American engineers, production systems are experiencing fundamental shifts in forms of organization and production. Three primary engines of change are driving these shifts: automation, telecommunications, and the changing nature of the relationships governing those subject to management and supervision. Computer systems have deeply affected the nature and types of work, significantly reducing elementary tasks and threatening to substitute for jobs, which, while of a higher order, may eventually be subject to automatization. The remarkable development of telecommunications has largely eliminated the need for close physical proximity, even for teams requiring a high degree of coordination. At the same time, in the more technically and scientifically advanced workplaces, the nature of organization has changed as the dominance of highly skilled professionals has come to blur distinctions between supervisory roles and other work categories. Ellis goes on to note (pp. 13 and 18) that

> Like all historic social forces, globalism is a mixed blessing. A great world culture is emerging, in which educated people everywhere share common interests. There is a potential for a vast expansion of the pool of talent and thus for the creation of new human capacities. But the process of change entails its friction, and some people do not fare well. As educated workers from formerly obscure countries arise to claim their share of the available work, those who were doing the work before must either compete or retire. If the total amount of work to be done grows fast enough to accommodate

increases in the size of the pool of talent, this situation presents no serious problems . . . [but] there is a real possibility that the supply of work will not keep up with the supply of workers . . . the world-wide spread of decent educational systems, from primary grades to an increasing number of third-world universities, means that highly skilled people can be found everywhere . . . Like it or not, we must all now compete in a much bigger arena if we wish to survive as practitioners of state of the art technical disciplines.

In a global economy, then, even the jobs of highly skilled American workers can be at risk since equally skilled professionals in other countries can act as cheaper and equally efficient substitutes, as has occurred in many mature industries dominated by blue-collar workers. On the other hand, the nature of high-tech industries is such that companies, as Keely (1998:31) observes, do not operate under the assumption that "labor is largely substitutable." Firms seek very specific knowledge and do not have enough time to develop in-house expertise by training current employees in new technological processes. With intense global competition and rapid production cycles, failure to hire workers with the proper skills could well translate into losses in competition and forfeited business opportunities.

One response to growing competitive pressures and the internationalization of knowledge is skilled immigration. This is certainly true in the United States, where, among some economic sectors, skilled immigration is seen as contributing to the country's scientific and technical lead in many industries. Highly skilled immigration is facilitated to a great degree, of course, by the internationalization of common knowledge, values, and attitudes. Countries most closely identified with the American system of higher education are more likely to provide skilled immigrants. Cheng and Yan (1998: 634), in their study of factors driving skilled immigration to the United States, conclude,

The articulation of higher education across countries provides similar training of skills, shapes common universal values, facilitates transnational ties, and therefore produces a large pool of internationally employable professionals. Since the extent of educational articulation between the sending country and the United States differs, the level of professional immigration . . . also vary. . . . The evidence clearly corroborates that economic and educational interactions between sending and receiving countries are important driving forces of professional migration. As the degrees of economic interaction and educational articulation between the sending country and the United States heighten, the level of highly trained migration to the United States rises.

For years, many proponents of immigration reform, aware of these educational developments and seeking to take advantage of the growing pool of highly skilled professionals overseas, have advocated a paradigmatic shift in the selection of migrants. This was partly achieved through the 1990 Immigration Reform Act when added emphasis was given to skill-based labor market criteria in the selection of migrants, although this piece of legislation did not downplay the importance of family relationship criteria in immigrant admissions. Regardless of what this legislation achieved, during the last decade the admission of highly skilled temporary and permanent immigrant workers to the United States has generated considerable controversy. The genesis of the debate is rooted in a broader national dialogue concerning the role of immigration in American society that encompasses varying perceptions about the types and numbers of immigrants the nation ought to welcome.

The controversy includes conflicting viewpoints regarding the admission of university-trained scientists and engineers, including those at the doctoral level. Some commentators have called attention to the economic gains arising from such immigration, pointing out that it brings to U.S. shores some of the brightest, best-educated, and most productive workers in the world. They further assert that in a global economy the temporary admission of skilled foreign workers provides firms with needed flexibility by allowing them to address spot shortages of very specialized skilled workers (Keely 1996; Papademetriou 1996). As summarized by Lowell (1996:11),

> Global firms and fast evolving, knowledge-based products demand a very different perspective than yesterday's. Today's knowledge industries must be fast moving and their product, unlike yesterday's industries, does not become more expensive to produce as raw materials are used—a process that takes time. By extension, today's knowledge industries cannot treat all workers as essentially interchangeable; training takes time and may never fully compensate for a foreigner's specialized experience in a desired foreign market. Contemporary knowledge industries face steep, up-front development costs that are recouped by volume (and ever cheaper) sales, and the race for market share goes to those who get their product out first. Getting the right worker with specific qualifications for short-term needs can be very important in these competitive marketplaces.

Some observers, while acknowledging the positive contributions skilled immigrant workers make to the U.S. economy, including the flexibility they provide industry, note that their presence in the American labor market, in some instances, can harm U.S. workers. If foreign workers are concentrated in certain areas of the economy, or where there is an oversupply of skilled workers, the temporary or permanent admission of skilled foreign workers can dampen employment and earnings prospects for U.S. resident workers (North 1996; DeFreitas 1996).

Fueling the debate is the perception that in some sectors of the economy there is a growing and perhaps excessive supply of skilled professional workers whose employment prospects are deeply influenced by cyclical shifts in labor demand. During the early 1990s recession, for example, the country experienced a major decline in demand for highly skilled workers, including engineers and natural scientists. The contraction in demand was aggravated by other factors, including the end of the Cold War and the resulting downsizing of the defense industry—as well as, according to some—globalization of the world economy.

Temporary versus Permanent Immigration

Much of the argument about highly skilled immigration is also based in conflicting views regarding the impact that the temporary entry of workers, of whatever kind, should have on the admission of permanent residents, and what this implies for American workers. Some critics feel that the current mechanisms utilized for regulating the entry of temporary foreign workers into the U.S. labor market undermine the rules designed to admit permanent immigrants and protect American workers. By virtue of their U.S. labor market experience, workers admitted with temporary work visas increase the likelihood of gaining a permanent foothold in the American labor market. With an eye toward eventually gaining permanent residency, these same critics note, skilled workers admitted under short-term visas are willing to accept lower wages and poorer working conditions than are U.S. workers, thus potentially affecting adversely the wages and working conditions of Americans.

Visa status changes, however, as some observers have remarked, are consistent with current immigrant admission rules which *de facto* reward temporary immigrants who possess successful U.S. labor market work histories. On the other hand, the use of temporary employment visas can cause problems if unscrupulous employers use them to import temporary workers to undercut prevailing wage rates, thus making a negative impact on the employment conditions of U.S. workers (Keely 1996; North 1996; Papademetriou 1996).

Foreign Graduate Education in the United States

Another important element of the debate has centered on the role of the graduate education of foreign students in the United States. The issue here, more specifically, is the eventual U.S. labor market impact when foreign graduate students join the U.S. workforce, or, after completing their studies, adjust to a temporary work visa category (e.g., H–1B). Over the last several decades, the number of foreign graduate students in American universities has risen markedly, particularly for doctoral students in engineering and the natural sciences, whereas the total number of U.S. doctoral scientists has remained relatively constant.

A frequently made observation is that graduate education in engineering and the sciences holds limited appeal for U.S. students because of the considerable time commitment, intellectual effort, anticipated career earnings, and actual and opportunity costs of graduate education in these fields. The contrast is made with the study of law, medicine, or business (see North, 1995 for a review of these perspectives), where the potential financial payoff is significantly higher and more immediate. The limited appeal to U.S. students to pursue graduate degrees in engineering and the sciences has placed many undergraduate and graduate programs—a large proportion of which were created or expanded as recently as the 1960s and 1970s—in a quandary. These programs would not be able to continue operating without graduate students, either as research or teaching assistants, and eventually as postdoctoral students or faculty, in the absence of an alternate graduate student pool. Dresch (1987) cogently summarizes this view when he notes,

> The continued growth of undergraduate enrollment has resulted in substantial demands for faculty, while domestic students have been deterred from graduate education and faculty careers by the relative attractiveness

of nonacademic employment, with the result that foreign students consti-
tute the primary source of supply of graduate students but also of new
faculty recruits. . . . Not fortuitously, the supply of foreign graduate students (and subsequently, faculty) to the academic system has been highly
responsive. (4)

Foreign students have helped fill the void left by U.S. students, thus
assuring the survival of numerous graduate programs. Universities,
likewise, have increasingly relied on the expanding pool of highly
skilled and often U.S.-trained foreign graduates to fill academic jobs
at American higher education institutions. Foreign students are motivated to seek graduate science and engineering degrees because in
many countries (including developing nations), the pursuit of a graduate education in these fields—contrary to what has happened in the
United States—continues to be regarded as prestigious and financially
rewarding. Further, some of the best students from these countries
(e.g., India, Mainland China) may in fact see science and engineering
degrees as permanent emigration tickets to developed countries (Rao
1995).

Graduates from prestigious Indian universities, for example, are not
only likely to be accepted as graduate students in American universities, but are also more likely to adjust to permanent residence status in
the United States once they complete their graduate education. Bhagwati
and Rao (1996) claim that America benefits immensely by welcoming
as immigrants these top graduates of foreign universities. In their view,
the growing presence of foreign graduate students in American universities is not simply a result of the avoidance of graduate education by
American students. Rather, it reflects the "meritocratic and nondis-
criminatory" admission policies of U.S. universities and the fact that
the overall quality and number of foreign student applicants has increased dramatically in past decades.

Overproduction of Ph.D.s

Proponents of the "Ph.D. glut" thesis argue that the American graduate education system has in fact produced far more doctorates in some
fields that the U.S. economy can productively absorb. They note, for
example, that the unemployment rate among recent doctoral-level math-
ematicians and physicists runs between 12 and 20 percent, and that

many of these highly skilled professionals are eventually forced to take jobs outside their fields (Zacher 1997). These observers place the blame for the overproduction of scientific doctorates squarely on university departments needing to maintain the required number of doctoral students to sustain their teaching and research requirements, since these students provide essential and affordable graduate assistance. Generous federal foreign-student training and immigration policies, and the attractiveness of the U.S. labor market for foreign nationals, they argue, ensure that graduate student education slots are always occupied in U.S. universities, whether by American or international students. The excess availability of scientific doctorates benefits industry and the universities by creating a buyer's market for scientific talent, while forcing many with new doctorates to deal with underemployment, labor insecurity, and low salaries.

Matloff (1997), for example, when discussing the role of immigrant workers in the computer field, the scientific arena that has attracted the most attention, concludes that

- The primary reason the foreign students join U.S. graduate programs in computer science is not because they seek the education itself, but rather because they use it as a stepping stone to immigration to the United States;
- [The United States does] not need to have so many foreign students in computer science Ph.D. programs—nor so many domestic students. [The United States] is greatly overproducing Ph.D.'s in the field;
- Though some of the foreign students in computer science graduate programs are of exceptionally high intellectual caliber, most are only of ordinary talent;
- The vast majority of major technological advances in the computer industry have been made by U.S. natives;
- The computer software industry is incorrect in its claim that it needs to hire large numbers of foreign nationals to remedy labor shortages in the field. There is no shortage of programmers; and
- Many computer industry employers exploit the foreign nationals they hire, by paying them lower salaries.

Thus, Matloff's conclusions rest on two basic premises. One is that many U.S. employers, including universities, take advantage of the desire of many foreign computer scientists to settle in the United States by paying them less than U.S. workers. Immigrant workers are content with the situation in any instance; although they are paid less than their American counterparts, U.S. salaries are much higher than in their home countries. The second premise is that the contribution of these immigrant workers to the U.S. economy is far less than claimed by skilled-immigration proponents; as a group, immigrant computer scientists are neither exceptionally talented nor have they made disproportionate contributions to technological developments.

North (1995:124), while acknowledging that foreign-born science and engineering graduate students have provided major benefits to American higher education, concludes that their presence on American campuses has had several little-noticed effects. One of these is that they have allowed universities and society at large to avoid urgently needed but painful adjustments while preserving the status quo. Given the ever-expanding pool of foreign graduate students, universities have not been forced to cut back programs because of the reduced demand from native-born students; there was no need to press strongly to recruit (although some of this is done) from among nontraditional potential American sources of science and engineering graduate students, such as women and resident minorities; and there was no need to make significant increases in graduate school stipends or postdocs' salaries (124–125).

All these developments have had a detrimental impact on the American scientific work force. North (p. 124) notes as well that the expanding supply of foreign graduate students has allowed continued growth in the number of graduate departments (as well as in the overall number of graduate students). The end result is continued expansion of the supply of advanced degree recipients, not all of whom can readily find employment. Another consequence is that major research universities have been able to shift more government grant money to overhead accounts, rather than to the pockets of graduate assistants, thereby partly accounting for the very low stipends of graduate students. Finally, "some displacement of native-born citizens" seeking graduate school admission has occurred partly as a result of the impressive increase in the number of highly qualified foreign applicants to graduate school. North cites, for example, an estimate by Finn that finds that for every four foreign-born engineering applicants accepted into graduate school, a native applicant is rejected.

Some concern has been expressed that minority applicants have been among those U.S. students most adversely affected. While the evidence on this point is not entirely clear, there are some indications that at the undergraduate level "crowding out through affirmative action targets occurs at colleges that are selective or very selective—with average SAT scores in excess of 1,100. Particularly important in this crowding out are nonresident aliens, who—in selective schools—are largely individuals on student visas" (Hoxby 1998:304). By virtue of their "minority" status, foreign students, in other words, substitute for American minority students for whose benefit affirmative action programs were designed and help colleges and universities to attain their minority enrollment targets.

A contesting explanation is that while there is in fact a "Ph.D. glut," it exists only within the halls of academe. The demand for doctoral-level professionals in universities, the traditional and historically preferred destination for Ph.D. scientists, has not kept pace with growth in the number of U.S.-produced doctorates. Several reasons have been cited for this development. Since the late 1970s, the number of vacant academic-track positions has been limited. One reason is that the rate of growth of college students has stabilized or declined because of the aging of the baby-boom birth cohorts. Further, many of the Ph.D.s hired during the period of rapid university expansion—the 1960s and 1970s—are still on the job and will not retire for at least one or two more decades. In addition, the increase in the total number of doctorates has aggravated pressures on an already-saturated academic labor market. These trends explain why very often academic job announcements in the sciences result in hundreds of applications being received by recruiting universities.

When assessing labor market demand for science doctorates as a whole, that is, by combining academic employment with employment in government and industry, a more mixed picture emerges. In some fields (e.g., chemistry), unemployment rates are generally low, and even during economic recessions they remain manageable. In contrast, in fields such as mathematics and physics there are strong reasons to believe that there is a doctorate oversupply, not unlike that which has plagued the humanities and social sciences for the last several decades.

Economic Cycles and Shifts in Skilled-Labor Demand

Recent economic developments have called into question some of the premises of those analysts who have concluded that the United

States has to contend with an across-the-board excess supply of graduate scientists and engineers. While there are grounds to think that there is an oversupply in selected fields (e.g., mathematics and physics), there is mounting evidence that in other fields (e.g., computer science and electrical engineering) perceptions of excess supply have been colored to some extent by the effects of economic cycles. With the American economy roaring by the mid-to-late 1990s, demand for most categories of highly skilled workers rose phenomenally. Most remarkable has been the surge in demand for computer programmers. It was often said in the early 1990s that the United States was facing a severe glut of computer scientists and that temporary immigrants with computer skills were depressing wages and displacing American workers. Some observers held that immigrant computer scientists were being admitted not because of a shortage of U.S. computer scientists, but because industry wanted a larger and cheaper pool of computer programmers. The graduate education policies of American universities were also blamed for contributing to the glut by overproducing computer scientists, many of whom were foreign nationals pursuing academic degrees in these fields to help them obtain permanent U. S. residence (Matloff 1997).

These claims came under fire in 1998 and 1999, with the press reporting that many employers were busily recruiting competent computer programmers in any country where they could be found with offers of temporary work visas and highly competitive wages (ranging from $48,000 to $64,000 a year, plus bonuses). The shortage of computer programmers and electrical engineers has been described as severe, with "more than 190,000 programming and other computer jobs" unfilled, according to a 1997 survey by Information Technology of America, a business trade group. By early 1998, the unemployment rate among electrical engineers had dipped to 0.04 percent. Seventy percent of the high-technology companies interviewed for the survey reported that a dearth of trained employees was interfering with corporate growth (Kaufman 1998:1). The president of Cypress Semiconductor Corporation, a leading electronics firm, claimed (*Wall Street Journal*, March 9, 1998: A–18) that because of the firm's inability to access foreign skilled workers (because the 65,000 cap on H1-B visas had been reached), "four key projects had to be interrupted . . . delaying the sale of millions of new chips and the creation of hundreds of manufacturing jobs."

In late 1998, under intense industry pressure, Congress increased the annual H1-B visa cap (almost doubling it to 110,000 visas a year) to allow for the more expeditious entry of computer programmers and other skilled foreign workers. By mid–1999, all available H–1B visas had been allocated, and the business community was again knocking at the door of Congress clamoring for more. Allegations of fraudulent use of the H–1B program continue to be heard, however. There are claims that despite the booming economy, unscrupulous employers continue to rely on temporary foreign migrants in order to undercut the wages and working conditions of U.S. workers (Valbrun 1999).

The Biomedical Sciences and Biotechnology

Caskey (1996) and many others have described the enormous scientific advances that have led to the biomedical and biotechnology revolution that has unfolded at the end of the twentieth century. From the time Watson and Crick discovered the structure of the DNA molecule in 1953 until today, the pace of scientific discovery has grown exponentially, and many observers anticipate that the rate at which scientific and technical breakthroughs will occur in years to come will only accelerate further. Most importantly, the scientific discoveries of the laboratory are giving way to hitherto undreamed of therapeutic (e.g., genetically engineered drugs, gene therapy) and genetic engineering advances (e.g., the ability to clone animal and vegetable species) that are being reported in a seemingly unending stream of newspaper headlines.

Many of the scientific advances in basic life science knowledge over the last thirty years have been attributed to the funding made available by the U.S. government to national basic science research facilities and university-based laboratories across the country, especially for biomedical research. McKelvey (1996:96) has noted, however, that although many of the most significant breakthroughs have been achieved by U.S.-based scientists, these achievements have been dependent on the cumulative work of the international research community. As she points out, "much of the foundation of knowledge necessary for genetic engineering had previously been developed in Europe, and many younger European scientists worked in the United States and contributed to those scientific developments."

The growth in funding for biomedical research made available by the U.S. Congress through NIH has been exceptional, rising from $26 million in 1945 to $4 billion in 1988 constant dollars (Dustira 1992:37). In fiscal year 1997, Congress appropriated an NIH budget of $12.7 billion. American universities have also increased their expenditures in all areas of research, with industry contributing by 1992 approximately 8 percent of the total overall research budget (Schultz 1996:133), and the remainder coming from federal, state, and private sources. Basic research, including biological and biomedical research, is highly concentrated: 100 research universities receive approximately 85 percent of research funding, with the top ten research universities receiving the bulk of the funds.

The federal government's allocation of funds for biomedical research and development (including about 20 percent for the development of biotechnology techniques) has been mostly (about two-thirds) managed through programs operated by NIH. The trends in sources of funding for biomedical research began to gradually change in the late 1970s, with the share of federal funding for biomedical research and development declining as industry support increased (Dustira 1992:32 and 35). According to estimates released by the Institute for Biotechnology Information (Dibner 1997:575), in 1997 biotechnology firms spent $10 billion for research and development. These trends are consistent with the expansion of the biotechnological industry and the growing commercialization of new pharmaceuticals.

Properly speaking, as noted by the Office of Technology Assessment (U.S. Congress: Office of Technology Assessment 1991:3) in an oft-quoted report, "biotechnology is not an industry. It is, instead, a set of biological techniques, developed through decades of basic research, that are now being applied to research and product development in several industrial sectors." In these industrial sectors, major life science discoveries are predicted to revolutionize production methods and what is produced. The formal creation of the biotechnology industry is traced back to 1976 when Genentech, a pioneer firm in this sector, was established in California by bringing together scientists and venture capitalists (McKelvey 1996:92). Major agricultural advances are anticipated—many, in fact, are already a reality—as scientists gain the ability to develop disease—or plague-resistant transgenic plants, and— as through cloning or other biotechnological processes— they manage to replicate biologically identical specimens with the most desirable commercial traits. Equally extraordinary advances have been achieved in bioremediation, as scientists explore new, promising technologies to cope with growing environmental concerns (Parkin 1996).

As noted by the Office of Technology Assessment (U.S. Congress: Office of Technology Assessment 1991:3),

> The United States has led the world in the commercial development of biotechnology because of its strong research base—most notably in biomedical sciences—and the ability of entrepreneurs to finance their ideas. During the early 1980s, a combination of large-scale federal funding for basic biomedical research, hype surrounding commercial potential, and readily available venture capital funding led to the creation of hundreds of dedicated biotechnology companies.

The most rapid commercialization of products arising from the technological application of new life science knowledge has occurred in the pharmaceutical industry, where, by the mid–1990s, global sales of biotechnology products already exceeded $200 billion (Tomlinson 1996:63). This industry is at the apex of the modern global scientific enterprise and possesses multiple international linkages. As described by the Office of Technology Assessment (U.S. Congress: Office of Technology Assessment 1991:7–8),

> The modern pharmaceutical industry is a global, competitive, high-risk, high-return industry that develops and sells innovative high-value-added products in a tightly regulated process. Because of the strong barriers to entry which characterize the global pharmaceutical industry, many DCB [dedicated biotechnological companies] are focusing on niche markets and developing biotechnology-based pharmaceutical products. Established pharmaceutical companies have been increasingly developing in-house capabilities to complement their conventional research with biotechnological techniques for use as research tools. Strategic alliances and mergers between major multinational pharmaceutical companies and DBCs allow both to compete in the industry and combine their strengths: the innovative technologies and products of those DCBs with financial and marketing power blended with the development and regulatory experience of the major companies.

The complexity and high costs associated with developing and commercializing biomedical and biotechnology products result in the development of complex links between universities and federal research facilities, as well as intricate webs of strategic alliances among firms and universities, through which those involved obtain capital, know-how, access to new products and technologies, regulatory experience, marketing capacity, and so forth. According to *Biotechnology Guide U.S.A.*, the almost 1,100 biotechnology firms and 233 diversified companies in the industry are interconnected through thousands of licensing agreements, marketing agreements, and research contracts, often with university laboratories. In 1997, biotechnology-related firms were estimated to employ more than 312,000 workers, exclusive of a similar number of students, postdoctoral researchers, and technicians working at academic research laboratories (Dibner 1997:571–586). Research and development (R&D) employment in pharmaceutical firms increased by close to 5 percent between 1984 and 1988, with about two-thirds of the industry workers being classified as scientific or professional (Dustira 1992:45).

An indication of the commercial perils and successes of biotechnology is the fluidity that characterizes this sector. Many successful start-up firms are acquired or absorbed by large and well-financed multinational pharmaceutical firms, while others cease operations when they run into financial problems because of difficulties in development or marketing. Records maintained by the Institute for Biotechnology Information indicate that close to 800 biotechnology firms have been lost since the industry first became established in the 1970s. The typical small start-up biotechnology firm must spend anywhere between $5 and $10 million before bringing its first product to market, a process that usually takes between five and twelve years (Dibner 1997:581).

While progress in this field has been extraordinary, there is still much ground to cover because scientists are just beginning to develop a clear understanding of genetic functions and how genes interact with the environment and the aging process to induce unhealthy states. Another major hurdle is how to assure quality control in large-scale production processes as biological materials developed under carefully controlled laboratory conditions become industrialized (Shuler 1996:103).

Further major advances are anticipated in the biological sciences as the research focus continues to shift to interdisciplinary efforts capable of unlocking the mysteries of life. A National Science Foundation (1995) workshop concluded that

The great challenge and opportunity for biological science as we move into the 21st century is to understand biological systems in all their complexity while preserving and exploiting biological systems in a sustainable fashion. The tools for dealing with this complexity will require the adaptation and application of emerging technologies not only from biology, but also from many other fields of science and engineering. There is a pressing need to take advantage of and develop new analytical tools at all levels—from the molecular to the cellular, the system, the organism, and the community of organisms. The key will be to blend leading-edge biology with the appropriate technologies. In some cases the technology itself will be the leading edge. In other cases, the "right" technologies will be ones that have already been proven in other fields but whose application to biology is novel. In still other areas, the biological sciences could be the first users or might provide the original impetus to new technology development.

One such field is computational biology, an area that is receiving extensive research support from the federal government, particularly through NIH. Computational biology entails the use of advanced computer, mathematical, and information sciences to address biological questions requiring large-scale computation and analysis (Clutter 1996).

A major impetus behind the rapid expansion of the biotechnology industry was the Patent and Trademark Laws Amendment of 1980 (Public Law 96–517), also known as the Bayh-Dole Act, whereby universities were granted the right to patents for discoveries made with government funding. This was paralleled by the emergence of biotechnology-dedicated industries, often staffed with former or current university faculty. As described by Schultz (1996:140), the rationale behind the Bayh-Dole Act (see also Vaughan et al. 1992) was that

> Billions of dollars of federal funds had been spent in sponsoring research at universities and few jobs had resulted, and legislators were looking for ways to put technology into practice. The federal government had been particularly ineffective at marketing intellectual property (patents) that came from their research support in universities. By giving universities commercial rights to their research innovations, it was expected that it would be in the best (financial) interest of the universities to promote technological transfer in industry. Thus more effective methodologies for commercialization and job creation would evolve.

In some respects, the act, and how universities have accommodated to it, has generated controversy (e.g., claims that it would alter the traditional education and research mission of universities). The consensus is, however, that the Bayh-Dole Act has contributed to a major increase in cooperative ventures between universities and industry, particularly in the biotechnology sector, both among major multinational pharmaceutical firms (e.g., Hoechst, Smith Kline Beckman) and smaller technology-intensive start-up companies. A concurrent development has been the rapid increase in the number of university-industry research centers, particularly since the 1980s (Schultz 1996:143).

The Bayh-Dole Act also allowed small businesses and nonprofit organizations to benefit from patents acquired with federal funding. Similar provisions were gradually extended to large private entities engaged in government-sponsored research and to contractors operating government-owned research facilities, and, finally, through the enactment of the Federal Technology Transfer Act of 1986, to research being performed under agreements between government agencies and private industry (Eisenberg 1996:165–166; Chen 1992). The response among federally supported research facilities was swift. By 1991, for example, NIH had established "an Office of Technology Transfer, had developed 140 cooperative research and development agreements (CRADAs) with industry, had received about $3 million in royalties, and had relaxed its policies to permit NIH scientists to engage in compensated consulting for industrial organizations" (Malone 1992:27).

Foreign Biomedical Scientists and the U.S. Economy

The rapid expansion of the biotechnology industry and associated demand for technically trained personnel gave rise during the early 1990s to the emergence of what was regarded then as an impending paucity of life scientists. Vaughan et al. (1992:66 and 68) provided a typical assessment of the situation:

> Shortages of trained scientists are already a problem for some companies; the difficulty is expected to worsen. Particularly worrisome for biomedical companies are shortages of specialists such as pharmacologists, enzymologists, and toxicologists. A 1989 survey published by the NRC [National Research Council] showed shortages of these specialists in the double digits as a percentage of those employed.

By the end of the decade, however, this assessment was being called into question. Evidence was accumulating that young life science Ph.D.s were having difficulty in securing permanent research career positions, largely because of the reduced availability of faculty slots at universities and positions at federal labs, and a slowing down of hiring by industry (National Research Council 1998).

A related issue is that despite the undisputed leadership of the United States in biotechnology, numerous alarms have been raised regarding the alleged potential for America to lose its preeminent status in this industry. Although a significant share of basic biological discoveries and biotechnological developments have been made in U.S. labs—and the bulk of research and development expenditures has been borne by the U.S. taxpayer and industry—the commercialization of new pharmaceutical products, for example, is often done by foreign firms. The concern is that the United States may forfeit potential commercial advantages in the international marketplace, as it did in the electronics industry during the 1970s and 1980s, when other nations benefited from basic inventions and processes developed in the United States that American firms failed to commercialize. Evidence that this was already occurring was signaled by the decline in the number of drugs developed by U.S. firms entering clinical trials, as well as by a reduction in spending for R&D since the 1970s (Vaughan et al. 1992:70–71).

Concern about maintaining America's international commercial preeminence in biotechnology is in many ways related to the presence of foreign scientists in U.S. universities and laboratories. Although there is general agreement that basic research is by definition an enterprise that does not recognize international borders and in fact benefits from cross-national exchanges, nonetheless some observers worry that other countries have disproportionately benefited or could potentially benefit by learning from the scientific breakthroughs achieved in the United States. A good deal of this learning occurs while foreigners are working with American colleagues in U.S. private and federal labs and universities. The case of Japan is instructive in this regard and has received some attention, and the situation may also be applicable to other countries, notably in Europe, that posses strong, highly competitive biotechnology and pharmaceutical industries.

Japanese industry, with support from its national government, has designated the development of the biotechnology industry as a top priority for the twenty-first century. This has been manifested in the government's provision of generous support for biotechnology research—despite overall cuts in government spending for R&D—and the emphasis given to the development of commercial applications (National Research Council 1992:17).

Japan's commitment to the development of its biotechnology industry appears to depend partly on the conscious decision to take advantage of the body of knowledge developed in basic biomedicine by scientists in the United States. As indicated by the National Research Council (1992:35), two out of three Japanese scientists spending more than one month in the United States in 1988 were engaged in biotechnology research, as compared to only one-third of U.S. scientists working in Japan. Further, out of a total of 1,800 foreign researchers at NIH in 1988, 450 were Japanese. Japanese firms, like those in other countries, are increasingly entering into joint ventures with knowledge-intensive U.S. firms, as well as establishing research and business relationships with U.S.-based firms and universities in order to gain access to cutting-edge U.S. scientific and technological know-how. The National Research Council (1992:52) has concluded that

> The danger is that, if conscious strategies are not develop by U.S. participants to increase inflows of technology from Japan and to expand marketing and sales in Japan, the net result of increasing technology linkages in biotechnology will be to create significant competition from Japan without strengthening the ability of U.S. firms to compete and commercialize technologies.

The other side of the coin, as noted above, is the concern of some analysts that the temporary presence of foreign scientists in U.S. laboratories often leads to permanent settlement in the United States. While their permanent settlement could be beneficial to the development of U.S. scientific prowess and technological development, the argument goes, it could have potentially injurious consequences for U.S. scientists by increasing the overall supply of scientists, thus adversely affecting working conditions and even generating unfair competition.

Training and Employment in the Biomedical Sciences

In the late 1990s, the job situation in the biomedical sciences in the United States resembled that for computer scientists and engineers, with unemployment rates being described in a 1997 Federation of American Societies for Experimental Biology (FASEB 1997:1) report as "extremely low." Unemployment rates for biomedical doctorates have historically remained at low levels (below 2 percent), although they have fluctuated in unison with the business cycle, reaching a peak during the recession of the early 1990s. During the 1970s and 1980s, according to the National Research Council (1998), biomedicine, like other scientific fields, saw major growth in the number of Ph.D.s awarded by U.S. universities, with degree recipients increasing by 70 percent between 1972 and 1995, from 3,449 to 5,878. Foreign students (citizenship figures only reflect self-reports of nationality status) accounted for much of the increase in new doctorates, the number of non-U.S. graduates rising from 552 to 2,031, by 268 percent. Growth in the number of U.S. citizen graduates was far more modest—34 percent—increasing by 940 between 1972 and 1995, from 2,806 to 3,746.

As in other science and engineering fields, the biomedicine Ph.D. employment distribution by type of place of work has experienced a notable shift during the last several decades. In 1995, barely a majority of U.S. citizens with biomedical doctorates continued to be employed in academic settings (53.2 percent), as compared to seven out of ten (66.5 percent) in 1973. The relative number employed by government (11.9 percent in 1973 and 10.4 percent in 1995) and by other employers (7.7 percent and 6.5 percent) had also declined, but by narrower margins. In contrast, the share working in industry had more than doubled, increasing from 13.9 to 29.9 percent. Other important trend information gleaned from National Science Foundation statistics revealed that the number of employed U.S.-citizen biomedical Ph.D. graduates holding postdoctoral appointments rose from 5.7 percent in 1973 to 9.7 percent in 1995. Although the relative rise in the number of Ph.D.s holding postdoctorate positions one and two years after award of degree was significant, increasing from 26.5 percent to 58 percent, the increases were dramatic among those three and four years, and five and six years post-Ph.D. The percent holding postdoctoral positions three and four years after graduation rose from 7.3 in 1973 to 32.1 percent in 1995, and the percentage for those possessing doctorates for five to six years increased from 2.2 to 15.5 percent. Ten years after Ph.D. award, less than 1 percent were holding postdoctoral positions. Trends were similar among postdocs in academic and non-academic positions, except that the percent of those employed in non-academic positions more than doubled between 1973 and 1995. The actual increases in the total number of biomedical postdocs were markedly undercounted, however, since the National Science Foundation figures did not include the considerable number of graduates of foreign universities holding comparable positions in the United States.

Several reasons have been offered to explain why the length of time in postdoctoral positions has increased so sharply. Perhaps the most important is that postdoctoral appointments are commonly used to gain more expertise, often in subject areas different from those in which Ph.D. students first specialize. As the stock of biomedical knowledge to be mastered has mushroomed, new doctorates find it necessary to broaden their education and acquire additional skills. Recent graduates also accept postdoctoral appointments as they wait for permanent positions, especially in universities where academic appointments are currently scarce.

Another important trend in the training of biomedical scientists has been the increasing amount of time required to complete a doctoral degree. It expanded by about two years during the 1980s and the first half of the 1990s. Whereas in 1980 it took seven years for a biomedical Ph.D. to graduate after receiving his or her baccalaureate degree, by 1995, 8.9 years were required (or from six to 6.9 years after enrolling in graduate school). Some of the increase appeared to be related to differences in "type" of university, in university funding sources, and in amount of time taken out for earning money. The thesis here is that in most biomedical fields, students enrolled in academic departments rated in the top quarter by reputation "complete their degrees in a more timely fashion" than those attending schools ranked in the bottom quarter (FASEB 1997:20). The better-rated programs have not only attracted the most competent students, but also offered financial support to most or all of their graduate students. The opposite has been true among the lesser-ranked schools. As the numbers of biomedical graduate programs and students have disproportionately increased in lesser-ranked schools, so has the average amount of time required for completing the doctorate.

Debate has continued about the number of biomedical doctorates U.S. universities should graduate and about the role of U.S.-educated and foreign-trained non-U.S. biomedical scientists in American universities and the labor force, but the evidence at hand in the mid–1990s suggested one important, although qualified, conclusion. That is that there was not an excess supply of biomedical doctoral scientists, but rather that the type of jobs to which most recent biomedical doctorate scientists aspired to were in relative short supply because of a large and growing demand. For example, several hundred individuals usually applied for any given tenure-track university faculty position, the preferred employment choice for most biomedical Ph.D. scientists (Sowers 1997, p. 2). Perkins (1996:1) summarized the situation as follows:

> We do have a major problem; namely, a problem of unrequited expectations of a career in academic science on the part of a large subset of Ph.D. graduates. This problem appears to be especially acute for the graduates of our most prestigious institutions. In addition, a potential problem is developing related to the characteristics of the subpopulations comprising the postdoctoral pool. We face the possibility of creating a group of scientists with a second class status who will be unable to enter the traditional bioscience career paths . . . the arguments behind the idea of an overproduction of biological science Ph.D.s by U.S. universities are based heavily on generalizations that fail to consider the heterogeneity of the graduating population of Ph.D. programs, the origins of individuals within the postdoctoral pool, and the compensating changes that already have occurred in the distribution of graduates within the job market.

Perkins (1996:26) went on to identify two major reasons why many biomedical doctoral graduates were unhappy with their career prospects. One was that the most prestigious research-intensive universities were highly selective regarding the recruitment of permanent faculty. As a general rule, they evinced a strong preference for offering appointments to graduates of similarly ranked universities. Moreover, students attending elite universities were "more likely to have their aspirations of an academic career encouraged by the faculty of those prestigious institutions because an academic career was their own anticipation and it has been satisfyingly fulfilled."

The problem was that the most prestigious universities—25 percent of all biomedical Ph.D.s graduated from only fifteen of these institutions—produced four to six times the number of new doctorates required to replenish the faculty stock of these same institutions. Further, Perkins noted that 80 percent of all domestically produced biomedical graduate faculty had received doctorates from only thirty-five major universities, although 235 schools offered Ph.D.s in at least one bioscience area. Because of the oversupply of highly qualified, newly minted doctorates, therefore, lesser-ranked universities also generally

recruited faculty from among graduates of the most prestigious research-intensive universities, thus obstructing the ability of those from
lesser-ranked institutions to obtain faculty positions. The obvious conclusion was, hence, that "the probability of finding a tenure-track position at a research-intensive university is very low even if one is a
graduate of a prestigious university and it is vanishingly small if one is
not."

By the late 1990s, a grimmer assessment of the labor market prospects being faced by young biological scientists was emerging. An
authoritative report released in 1998 by the Committee on Dimensions, Causes, and Implications of Recent Trends in the Careers of
Life Scientists of the National Research Council, based on the detailed
analysis of large longitudinal databases maintained by its Office of
Scientific and Engineering Personnel, confirmed the overall trends
described above. It actually went further by concluding that the number of life science doctoral graduates produced by U.S. universities
exceeded the demand for life science Ph.D.s generated by higher educational institutions, industry, and government. The study (National
Research Council 1998:79) concluded that the life sciences (including
agriculture) are

> a flourishing, productive research enterprise with little unemployment but
> with a workforce heavily concentrated in "training" positions, such as
> graduate students and postdoctoral fellows. The occupants of these posi-
> tions are taking longer to obtain their Ph.D.s; they continue their training
> after graduate school by assuming postdoctoral positions; their tenure in
> these postdoctoral positions is lengthening; and when they seek out perma-
> nent positions, they face stiff competition—hundreds of applicants for a
> single post. The net effect of those trends is an ever-growing accumulation
> of highly trained young scientists in positions that were intended to be
> transitional. Yet these very people are essential for the accomplishment of
> the research that has brought so much benefit to the nation and reputation
> to its life-science endeavor . . . the system is producing more Ph.D.s that
> can be absorbed into the permanent workforce, and [yet] these trainees are
> essential to the conduct of research in U.S. universities. . . . The current
> situation is the product of a linked education-research system that is in
> disequilibrium because of features that are intrinsic and structural, that are
> not confined to the life sciences but have parallels elsewhere in higher
> education, and that are likely to continue to produce the same outcomes . . .

The report pointed out that much of the problem could be attributed

Figure 2.1
Number of US Life-Science PhDs awarded annually,
by citizenship, 1963–1996

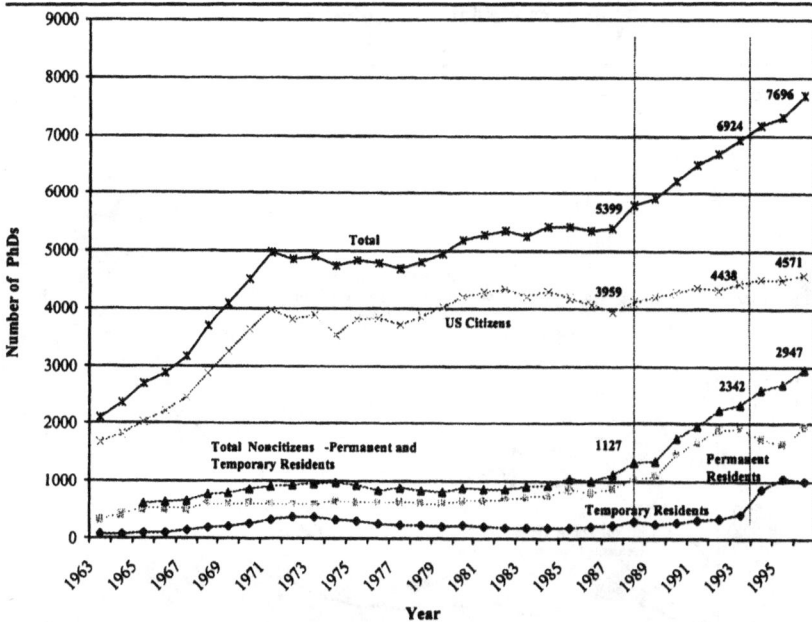

Source: National Research Council, 1998. *Trends in the Early Careers of Life Scientists.*
Washington, D.C.: National Academy Press. p. 23.

to the rising number of life science Ph.D.s awarded by U.S. universities to foreign nationals (as many as a quarter in some years), as depicted in figures 2.1 and 2.2. While recognizing that this development arises from the international prominence and reputation of U. S. life-science training and research, the Committee noted that for many foreign nationals "the low stipends paid to graduate students enable a higher standard of living for such applicants; and the prospect of a job or postdoctoral position and a permanent visa at the completion of graduate study is a powerful incentive for citizens of many countries." A direct implication is that at least some foreign life-science graduate students view their admission to U.S. universities and research labs as a roundabout way to settle in the United States (by by-passing more direct regular immigration mechanisms, such as applying for permanent residency status in consulates abroad). Thus, the training of foreign life scientists in the United States might to some degree be viewed

Figure 2.2
Number of US life-science PhDs awarded annually to
temporary residents and neumber and percentage of
temporary residents planning to remain in the
United States, 1963–1996

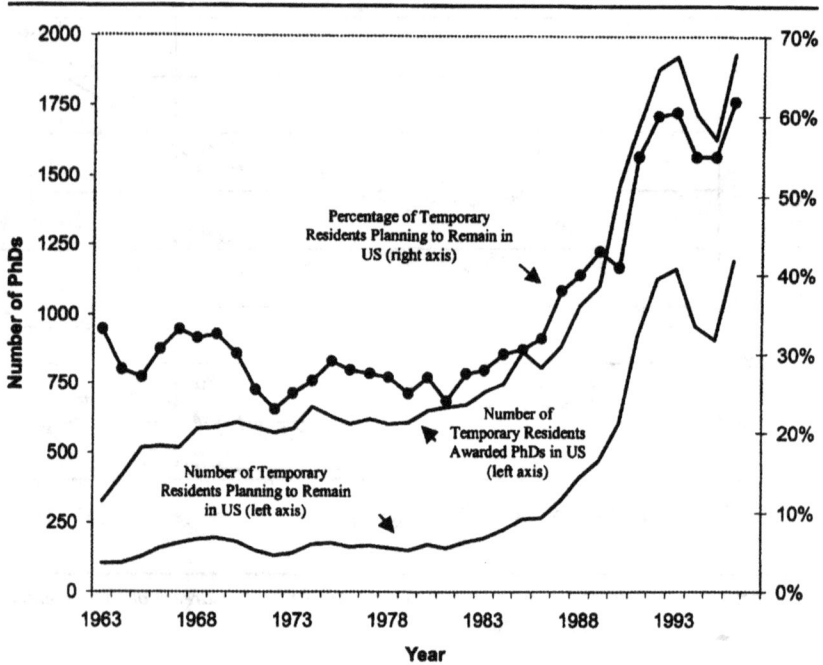

Source: National Research Council; *Trends In The Early Careers Of Life Scientists.* 1998;
Washington, DC; National Academy Press; p. 24

as having contributed to the labor market surplus of biomedical research scientists. An equally important observation was that aside from
the postdoctoral positions held by U.S.-trained foreign nationals in
American universities and laboratories, many more foreign postdocs
working in the United States had received their training abroad. In
total, about half of the 20,000 postdocs in the life sciences were foreign nationals.

The Committee on Dimensions, Causes, and Implications of Recent
Trends in the Careers of Life Scientists issued several recommendations to address the situation. The first and most important (pp. 80–82)
was to restrain the rate at which the number of graduate students in the
life sciences was increasing. This recommendation extended not only
to limiting student enrollments, but also to preventing the expansion or

establishment of new graduate education programs. The Committee also endorsed the notion (pp. 82–83) that prospective life science students be provided with accurate information regarding the employment prospects they are likely to face upon completing their training, including how earlier graduates have fared in the scientific labor market. Other Committee recommendations were that the educational experiences of life science graduate students be improved by providing them with more opportunities to pursue their own independent research agendas, as opposed to those of their mentors (pp. 83–85), and that the most scientifically promising graduates be presented with better financially compensated career transition options commensurate with their skills and prospective research futures (pp. 85–86).

The Committee recommended (pp. 86–88) that universities should continue treating the Ph.D. as a research-intensive degree, but that, at the same time, they should also consider identifying "specific fields of the life sciences for which master's-degree training is more appropriate, more efficient, and less expensive than Ph.D. training and that focused master's degree programs be established in those fields."

One final recommendation addressed the question of the role of foreign nationals in graduate education and postdoctoral fellowships. The Committee expressed concern that universities might respond to the earlier recommendations by increasing the number of foreign nationals in their classes and labs. While the Committee felt that it would be "unwise to place arbitrary limits on the number of visas issued for foreign students it did not believe that U.S. institutions should continue to enroll unlimited numbers of foreign nationals." Recommendation No. 7 of the Committee read (p. 89),

> If, as we hope, implementation of our recommendations results in constraining further growth in Ph.D.s awarded in the life sciences, we urge our colleagues on graduate admissions committees to resist the temptation to respond by simply increasing the number of foreign applicants admitted.

3

The National Institutes of Health

NIH is a unique research entity with a budget of $14.8 billion for the 1999 fiscal year. The NIH mission is

> To uncover new knowledge that will lead to better health for everyone. NIH works toward that mission by: conducting research in its own laboratories; supporting the research of non-federal scientists in universities, medical schools, hospitals, and research institutions throughout the country and abroad; helping in the training of research investigators; and fostering communication of biomedical information.

NIH is both similar to and different from academic institutions with which it has extensive research and training grant linkages, and which collectively represent a wealth of sources for NIH's recruitment of high-skilled talent. NIH is a biomedical research-oriented federal agency composed of many different semi-autonomous elements in its twenty-four institutes, centers, and divisions (ICDs), including the Warren Grant Magnuson Clinical Center, the National Library of Medicine, and the Fogarty International Center.

Structurally, and for purposes of the research activities it conducts or sponsors, the NIH is divided into two different programs: the Intramural and the Extramural. Through the former, the NIH conducts basic and clinical research at its 300-acre Bethesda, Maryland campus, as well as on several off-campus sites such as the Gerontology Research Center in Baltimore, Maryland, the Research Triangle Institute in North Carolina, the Rocky Mountain Laboratories in Hamilton, Montana, and facilities in Phoenix, Arizona.

The NIH staff totals some 14,000 employees conducting research, managing its Intramural and Extramural Research Programs, or providing other kinds of support. In 1994, for example, the Intramural Program included 1,100 tenured scientists, 250 staff scientists, 2,146 non-tenured scientists, 2,410 postdoctoral trainees, and 194 other trainees (National Institutes of Health 1995:5). Roughly 35 percent of those working at NIH are research scientists, with approximately one-third of the doctoral-level staff in the mid–1990s holding various types of non-immigrant visas, including 1,600 postdoctoral scientists with J–1 visas.

The scientists working in the NIH Intramural Program, which consists of more than 2,000 research projects and in 1996 received about 11 percent of NIH's budget, make important contributions to the basic knowledge upon which some of the most important advances in medical and dental care depend. The Intramural Program also plays a major domestic and international role in the training of numerous junior-level physicians and basic scientists who benefit from the research opportunities offered by NIH while engaged in short-to-medium term training and research appointments lasting from several weeks to a few years.

Through its Extramural Research Program, NIH has research contract and grant ties with many independent biomedical research and development entities in the United States and abroad. In the late 1990s, approximately 80 percent of NIH's financial resources were allocated for use by the Extramural Program to support research and training in more than 1,700 universities and research institutions in the United States and other countries. In 1996, the Extramural Program supported the work of 35,000 principal investigators in the United States as well as in several foreign countries. According to an article in the *Journal of NIH Research* ("Research Job Shortage" 1995:32), in 1995 NIH was planning to spend

> $565 million on individual and institutional research-training grants and research-career grants to support 15,456 budding biomedical scientists— $238 million and 3,241 trainees more than in 1985. A 1990 NIH survey suggested that roughly 9,000 more graduate students and postdocs are supported through NIH-funded research project grants.

The presence of NIH at its Bethesda campus in Montgomery County, Maryland, has fostered in this region an important biotechnology corridor which includes several important federal scientific research and administrative facilities, biomedical-related professional and philanthrophic organizations, and a growing number of privately owned biotechnology companies, many of which are staffed by former NIH employees and trainees. NIH serves as a readily accessible source of high-skilled scientific staff for these public and private entities. Among the latter are more than 230 biotechnology companies employing more than 42,000 workers that in 1995 were awarded upward of $221 million in contracts by NIH. These companies, averaging 100 employees in size, are engaged in diverse research and development activities, ranging from the cataloguing of genetic information, to developing advanced gene therapies and medical and pharmaceutical products, to innovative testing and laboratory services.

In addition to NIH, Montgomery County is home to the Food and Drug Administration, the U.S. Naval Hospital, Walter Reed Army Hospital, and the U.S. Armed Forces Medical School. This concentration of biomedical science-related federal institutions, together with close proximity to Washington, D.C., has contributed to the equally significant concentration of professional and philanthropic research organizations found in the vicinity of NIH. These include the American Red Cross, Holland Laboratories for the Biomedical Sciences, the United States Pharmacopeial Convention, the American Society for Human Genetics, the Howard Hughes Medical Institute, the American Society for Pharmacology and Experimental Therapeutics, and the Federation of American Societies for Experimental Biology, among many others. The presence in a limited geographic area of so many entities with an exclusive or predominant focus on biomedical research makes the region surrounding NIH an almost irresistible magnet to scientists the world over.

Selection of Biomedical Scientists and Conditions of Work at NIH

NIH seldom recruits foreign scientists for permanent employment at its intramural research facilities, although it occasionally sponsors highly promising non-U.S. scientists to fill selected tenured and nontenured staff positions. NIH mostly selects foreign nationals from a large pool of applicants for fixed and limited amounts of time to conduct research at its facilities as part of its mandate to promote "international cooperation in all aspects of the health sciences" (see

Appendix A[1] for an overview of training and research opportunities for foreign scientists at NIH as summarized from information provided at the NIH webpage). NIH fellowships or clinical associateships are time-limited research training and development opportunities offered to U.S. and foreign postdoctoral scientists. Upon completing their appointments, most postdoctoral fellows are expected to continue their careers elsewhere, whether in the United States or abroad.

Several programs, coordinated by the Fogarty International Center, the NIH's international arm, manage the temporary inflow of foreign scientists. The Fogarty International Center serves as the focal point for NIH's mission of "promoting international cooperation in all aspects of the health sciences," although "each NIH institute runs and funds its own intramural visiting scientists program" (Rhein 1990:74). This is in keeping with the traditionally recognized and growing appreciation of the "importance that is attached to international cooperation and exchange by many scientists" involved in the pursuit of biomedical research ("On Cabbages and Kings," 1997).

The programs administered by NIH include those that provide research experience and advanced training to foreign scientists in the United States, whether through the Intramural Program or the Extramural Program, as well as those designed to permit U.S. scientists to pursue research interests abroad. Among the latter are the Minority International Research Training Grant, the Senior International Fellowship, the Foreign-Funded Fellowships for U.S. Scientists Going Abroad, and the Summer Institute in Japan. The former include the International Training and Research Program in Environmental and Occupational Health, the International Training and Research Program in Population and Health, the International Research Fellowship, and the NIH Visiting Program. Most of these programs facilitate interactions between leading U.S. and foreign biomedical investigators (e.g., the Scholars in Residence Program, the International Studies Program, the International Research and Awards program) or promote the training of international researchers and health workers (e.g., International Research and Training in AIDS). The objectives and principal characteristics of the various Fogarty international programs are summarized in Appendix B.

The program most relevant to this study is the NIH Visiting Program, active since 1950. This program "provides talented scientists throughout the world an opportunity to participate in the varied research activities of NIH. Through this program, scientists at all levels of their careers are invited to NIH to receive further experience and to conduct cooperative research in their medical specialties" (NIH webpage). Applicants selected into the program receive funding from the U.S. government, including a stipend, and are placed (until early 1999) in one of three categories. Visiting Fellows (initially appointed for two years, with a one-year renewal option) are junior scientists with less than three years of postdoctoral research experience; Visiting Associates have between three and six years of postdoctoral experience; and Visiting Scientists have more than 6 years experience. While at NIH, the two senior categories of foreign scientists engage in collaborative research with their NIH U.S. counterparts.

Although Visiting Fellows receive a stipend from NIH, they are not considered its employees. This is not so for Visiting Associates and Visiting Scientists, who are regarded as NIH salaried employees. There are well-established procedures for foreign scientists to apply for positions under the NIH Visiting Program. These procedures are detailed in numerous publications as well as in the NIH webpage:

> Based on their credentials and research interests, foreign scientists are selected and invited by senior NIH scientists. To receive an invitation, foreign scientists must find an NIH scientist working in the same biomedical specialty in one of the NIH's intramural laboratories. An award or appointment to the NIH Visiting Program must be requested by the senior NIH scientist who serves as the participant's sponsor during his or her stay at NIH.

> Individuals interested in a Visiting Program fellowship award or appointment should write to an NIH senior scientist working in the same research field, enclosing a resume and brief description of their particular research area. Information about the research being conducted by NIH scientists and their names may be obtained from *the NIH's Scientific Directory and Annual Bibliography* . . .

These instructions are identical to those U.S. scientists must follow when seeking postdoctoral positions in NIH's Intramural Program, whether under the research or combined clinical and research pathway (for physicians and dentists).

While NIH as a rule does not recruit foreign scientists for permanent appointments, there are exceptional cases. As noted in *The NIH Catalyst*, an official NIH publication (Kolberg 1996:12),

Thanks to special authorities contained in the Public Health Service Act, NIH can hire the best available scientists for its tenure-track and tenured openings—even if those scientists happen to come from other countries. For example, two of the 26 people granted tenure by the Central Tenure Committee between June 1994 and October 1995 were foreign nationals. Furthermore, 33, or about 16 percent, of NIH's 201 tenure-track investigators are foreign nationals.

Gaining tenure or being placed on the tenure track does not instantly shift a foreign scientist into the same employment status as his or her American counterparts, however. Until tenured and tenure-track scientists become U.S. citizens—a process that usually takes at least five years after they become permanent residents and receive their green cards, they are still employed under the titles of "Visiting Associate" or "Visiting Scientist," rather than as General Schedule (GS) Civil Service employees, who must be U.S. citizens.

What is significant, however, is that the possible or actual U.S. research experience often acts as a mechanism that could potentially facilitate and ultimately lead to permanent settlement in the United States, whether under private sponsorship or a myriad of other mechanisms with such potential. Professional migration, in particular, and migration more generally—as documented in the extensive migration research literature—often follows from exposure to more promising career opportunities and the workings of intricate social networks that link individuals sharing similar occupational, ethnic, or professional characteristics. It follows, therefore, that in the pursuit of its international objectives, NIH sensitizes as well as exposes prospective migrants to the migration option, or actually serves as a vehicle that allows scientists wishing to migrate to implement their migration objectives.

Trend data on the distribution of postdoctoral trainees at NIH between 1987 and 1996 indicates that while the absolute number of foreign postdoctoral trainees increased by more than 20 percent (from less than 800 in 1987, to about 1,000 in 1996), during the intervening years, the number of U.S. fellows rose at a much faster rate, increasing by nearly 250 percent (from about 640 in 1987, to more than 1,600 in 1996). Whereas in 1987 there were more Visiting Fellows than U.S. Fellows, by 1996 the reverse was true, the number of U.S. Fellows exceeding by nearly a third the number of Visiting Fellows (See figure 3.1).

FIGURE 3.1
Postdoctoral Trainees at NIH, 1987 to 1996*

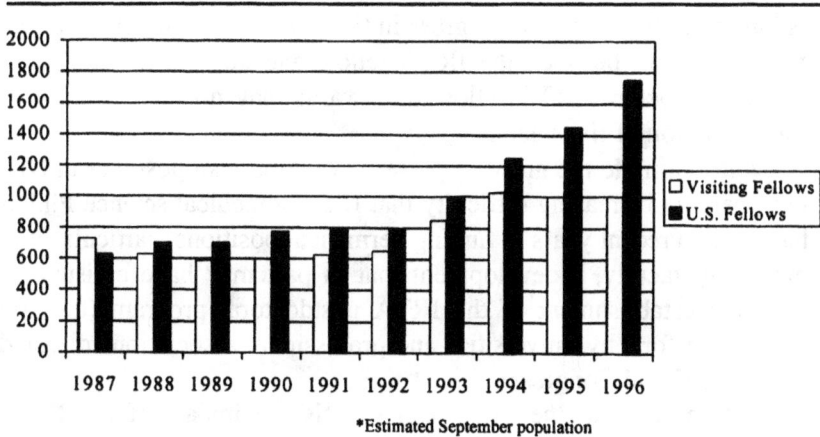

*Estimated September population

The reversal in the distribution of foreign and U.S. fellows can be explained by several factors, in part mediated by the rising federal funding trend for NIH. Most prominent among this was the establishment of NIH's Intramural Research Training Award Program (IRTA) for American postdocs in 1990 for the principal benefit of trainees to provide them with opportunities for developmental training and practical research experience in a variety of disciplines related to biomedical research, medical library research, and related fields. Service is a by-product of the IRTA Program.

IRTA Program participants must be U.S. citizens or permanent resident aliens. Acceptable proof must be presented at the time they report to activate their awards. There are five types of IRTA traineeships: 1) postdoctoral, 2) predoctoral, 3) postbaccalaureate, 4) technical, and 5) student.

To be eligible for a postdoctoral IRTA fellowship, an individual must possess a Ph.D., M.D., D.D.S., D.M.D., D.V.D. or equivalent degree in a biomedical, behavioral, or related science, or certification by a university as meeting all the requirements leading to such a doctorate; and 5 or fewer years of relevant postdoctoral experience and up to 2 additional years of experience not oriented towards research, such as clinical training for physicians.

IRTA fellowship commitments may be made for an initial period of either one or two years, with the potential for renewal, in increments of one year. Renewal of IRTA awards beyond the initial commitment is based on demonstrated progress in the training assignment and mutual agreement between the IRTA fellow and appropriate ICD officials. Postdoctoral IRTA fellowship awards may not exceed a maximum duration of five years.

Contributing to the growing presence of American postdocs at NIH has been the increasing difficulty that U.S. biomedical science Ph.D.s have had in recent years in finding permanent positions, particularly as university faculty, a development that in part may have assisted, in turn, the establishment of the IRTA postdoctoral program (through lobbying efforts by universities and professional associations directed toward NIH and Congress).

A closer look at the trend data reveals the impact of the IRTA program on the distribution of American and foreign postdoctoral trainees. As noted, the number of Visiting Fellows increased steeply between 1979 and 1986, rising from 391 to 736, or by 88 percent in an eight-year period, and then declined for the next four years (see figure 3.2). By 1989, Visiting Fellows numbers had dropped to 587. The first 263 IRTA postdocs arrived at NIH in 1990 as the number of foreign fellows again began to rise. By 1995, 947 IRTA postdocs were working side by side with 1,033 foreign Visiting Fellows, the number of

Figure 3.2
Trends in the Number of Visiting Fellows and IRTA Fellows at NIH,
1979 to 1995

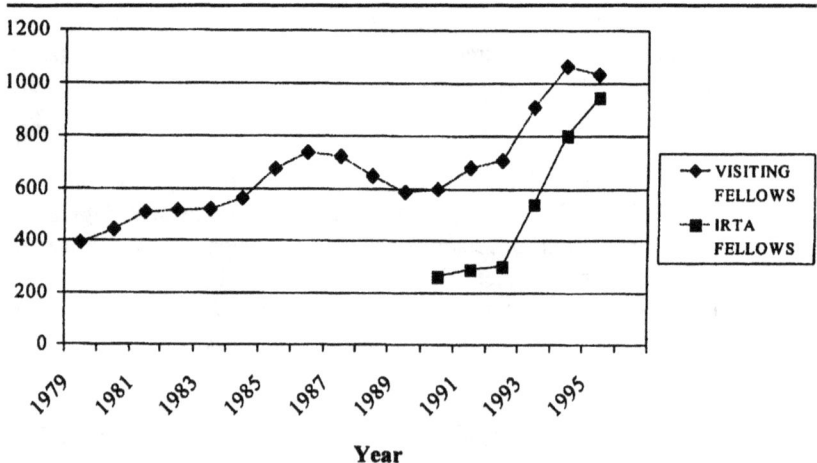

IRTA postdocs having increased by 260 percent during the interval as compared to 72 percent for the foreign postdocs. If considering together foreign visiting postdocs and IRTA postdocs, the number of postdoctoral slots at NIH increased by 1,589 between 1979 and 1995, by more than 400 percent.

Despite the increase in the number of American postdocs, there is anecdotal evidence suggesting that for young U.S. scientists an NIH postdoctoral appointment is not as prestigious today as it was in the past. For one thing, some observers have noted that NIH presently fails to attract established research scientists or loses to other entities some of its more promising young researchers because NIH salaries are "too low to attract [or retain] senior researchers" (Roberts 1991:21). In addition, postdoctoral appointments are not as attractive as they once were for three reasons (Caudle 1996). The first is that postdoctoral appointments at NIH are much too brief (normally three to five years) to develop sufficient professional recognition to land the most coveted academic jobs. The second is that given the nature of research funding at NIH (funded internally and not dependent on applying for and successfully winning research grants), postdoctoral fellows are not exposed to mentors with grant-writing skills; they fail, therefore, to acquire a much demanded skill in most university departments. The last and related reason is that often universities set as a pre-hiring requirement that new faculty bring their own research grants.

Of the 1,896 foreign biomedical scientists in residence at NIH in mid–1996 (as a general rule and on average, over 2,000 foreign scientists spend some time at NIH each year), as seen in Table 1, 1,524 (or 80 percent) were on NIH J–1 visas (issued to research scholars), while an additional 48 (2.5 percent) were on J–2 visas, the visas issued to dependents of exchange visitors.[2] The vast majority of the Visiting Fellows, accounting for 59 percent of all foreign scientists, had J–1 visas. Fifty-eight (3.1 percent) held ECFMG J–1 visas, a category reserved for alien research physicians.[3] O–1 visas (for aliens of extraordinary ability) were held by thirty-eight scientists (mostly Visiting Associates and Visiting Scientists), while a further thirty-two were at NIH on B–1 (visitors for business) visas. Some scientists (twenty-seven) were on EAD, a transitional category reserved for those in the process of moving from one visa status to another, with the remainder clustered in a few other visa types (twenty-nine on F–1, student visas; twenty-two on TN visas reserved for Canadians under the NAFTA

TABLE 3.1
NIH Visiting Foreign Scientists by Nonimmigrant Visa and NIH Program
(June 1996)

	ECFMG J-1 (Alien Physician)	NIH J-1 (Research Scholar)	J-2	H-1B	O-1	F-1	B-1	WB	TN	G-4	EAD	AI/A2	TOTAL:
Visiting Fellows	3	1056	12			17			14	1	11		1114
Visiting Associates/ Visiting Scientists	52	158	4	91	36	2			5	4	9		361
Guest Researchers/ Special Volunteers	1	232	23	11	2	9	24	3	2	3	4	2	316
Fogarty Scholar-in-Residence		7											7
Exchange Scientists	2	45	6				6	1			3		63
Special Experts Professional Services		1		2									3
Contract		12	2			1	2						17
General Fellows		4	1										5
Supplemental Fellows		9							1				10
TOTAL:	58	1524	48	104	38	29	32	4	22	8	27	2	1896

Source: Unpublished NIH Data.

treaty; and eight on G–4, visas for employees of international organizations). Of particular note was the fact that 104 foreign scientists, mostly Visiting Associates/Visiting Scientists and Guest Researchers/ Special Volunteers, were working at NIH with H–1B visas. H–1B visas by definition are granted to temporary workers admitted to the United States for periods of up to three years (renewable for an additional three years) to perform services in a specialty occupation, including medicine and health education. This visa is often used as a bridge between nonimmigrant and immigrant status.

The diversity of foreign scientist national origins at NIH and the manner in which this diversity has evolved over time can be appreciated by studying the data provided in Appendix D. These figures include all foreign scientists at NIH, regardless of temporary visa status. Since 1970, scientists from more than 100 countries have done research at NIH; in 1998, ninety-two foreign countries were represented. Slightly over one-quarter of the foreign scientists in 1998 (28.5 percent) were from developing countries, and the balance from the developed world, including recently industrialized Asian nations. The statistics in Appendix D can also be used to assess how the presence of foreign scientists at NIH has increased over time.

The ten leading foreign scientist source countries for 1998, as well as trends of increase for these countries, are shown in table 3.2. Japan

TABLE 3.2
Trends in the Number of Foreign Scientists at NIH for the Ten Leading Source Countries of Origin in 1998

Country	1970	1980	1990	1996	1998
Japan	51	199	351	318	332
China, People's Republic	2	10	188	269	326
Korea	1	12	47	91	147
Canada	4	41	52	93	135
Italy	14	71	139	149	132
India	9	114	103	104	126
Germany	13	18	63	132	119
Russia*				119	108
United Kingdom	24	82	109	84	106
France	2	27	63	75	90
All countries	199	985	1756	2097	2295

*Excludes scientists from the former Soviet Union before 1990. The number of scientists from the former Soviet Union and constituent republics may be found in appendix D.

Source: NIH unpublished data shown in Appendix D.

was first, followed by the People's Republic of China and the Republic of Korea. The list also includes four Western European countries and Canada, together with India and Russia. Since the 1990s, as may be noted in Appendix D, the number of foreign scientists from former Soviet Republics other than Russia and ex-communist Eastern European countries has also been on the rise.

Reasons for the Significant Presence of Foreign Biomedical Scientists at NIH and in the United States Generally

Current NIH administrators and scientists pointed out that NIH is a unique organizational entity: It is part of the federal government—of the U.S. Department of Health and Human Services—yet it is research oriented and has many similarities to academic institutions, including a tenure system. It was explained that NIH seeks scientists from abroad, usually in the form of postdoctoral trainees, partially because of NIH's mandate to promote international cooperation and knowledge in health, and partially because of the difficulty of acquiring a sufficient number of American scientists qualified in certain specialized areas. A major reason given for this situation was that not enough U.S. students are entering these fields because American culture does not place high value—or financial reward—on extended training, achievement of the Ph.D., and careers in scientific research.

Some alluded to the Reagan era efforts to downsize the federal government by implementing "reductions in force" that eliminated government employee positions. This impelled NIH, like other federal agencies trying to carry out their congressionally mandated functions, to increasingly outsource work under contract to private sector firms possessing skilled personnel, many of whom were foreign scientists. NIH's constituent institutes continue this practice.

Further, it was explained that NIH found another avenue for meeting the need for scientific personnel through its existing role as a training institution. The Fogarty International Center was established at NIH in 1968 for the purpose of advancing international cooperation and knowledge in health. However, at the outset the number of foreign scientists that the Fogarty Center brought to NIH's Intramural Research Program was rather small—199 in 1970. Yet the number of Visiting Fogarty Scientists, Associates, and Fellows has steadily increased since then: to 985 in 1980, 1,756 in 1990, and 2,295 by 1998.

The great majority of these foreign scientists hold J–1 exchange visitor visas that extend for three years and may be extended for a second three-year period. This visitor exchange program was financed through the United States Information Agency (USIA). In the 1990s, USIA was incorporated into the U.S. Department of State, whose Bureau of Educational and Cultural Affairs manages the program.

A number of explanations were offered by current NIH administrators and scientists as to why NIH invites foreign scientists for postdoctoral training. Some spoke with pride of NIH's mandate to forge international connections. By doing this, one person noted, the United States benefits, as when scientific knowledge regarding cellular immunology generated in Germany and Italy began to be utilized at NIH. In the view of this scientist, "science is international; diversity is good in itself." According to another interviewee,

"It is the culture of NIH to have an international ambiance and to foster international understanding. Further, depending on the scientific question under investigation, these existing international ties make it easy to bring in foreign expertise." This perspective was similar to that of a research immunologist with many years at NIH who explained that NIH brings in foreign postdocs

> To create diversity, which enriches the intellectual environment. NIH is trying to select the best people to make a contribution—biomedicine has no national boundaries. Training and work are combined; such is the social organization of scientific research. It is intended that training of foreign fellows at NIH will have a long-term positive effect in their home countries.

Several interviewees mentioned that international scientific exchanges mutually benefit scientists and the organizations they are associated with. Foreign scientists "bring their own ingenuity. They renew and invigorate NIH; these are young enthusiastic scientists. Without the influence of young and enthusiastic scientists, NIH would have lost its impetus and creativity. NIH's production of laureates, who worked with enthusiasm, is in part due to the presence of foreign scientists." One of these laureates, a biochemist, flatly declared, "They enabled me to win a Nobel Prize." The training programs are also viewed as politically beneficial for the United States. One senior staff fellow, a naturalized citizen born in China, mentioned, for example, "that foreign scientists [who had trained at NIH] eventually move up high in their governments, which gives the United States high influence on other governments." At the same time, according to a physician who directs a branch of one of the institutes, "foreign scientists come to NIH to take advantage of information and training they receive and can take back to their home countries. NIH provides a service; they learn and establish credentials that can be used back home."

A number of individuals also alluded to the use of foreign postdocs as an effective way in which NIH addresses manpower bottlenecks, manages to adhere to employment guidelines, minimizes research costs, and even reduces the moral obligation of mentors to find permanent employment for their trainees. According to a biochemist with seven years of NIH experience,

> There are a certain number of "slots" in the lab reserved for U.S. citizens. Bringing in a Fogarty fellow doesn't count as filling one of those "slots." So, you can get more bodies in your lab to do work. Normally foreign scientists are obliged to go home when their postdoc is over, so there isn't an obligation to place them like there is for American scientists. The job market in the United States is very difficult now. It used to be that you were a postdoc for 3–4 years, now it is up to ten. For a mentor in the lab, bringing in an American scientist brings in a moral, if not actual, obligation to place them in a job at the end of the postdoc. You don't have that with foreign students since they go back home.

The issue of lack of American scientific manpower came up repeatedly. One person commented that "U.S. M.D.s want to make money in a hurry, and postdocs' salaries are low." A molecular biologist, chief of one of NIH's labs, noted that the foreign postdocs make an important contribution to the institutes' workforce. "It is becoming more and more difficult," he observed, "for NIH to hire at the [postdoc] training level in the United States . . . due to paucity of numbers and to competition from other entities." NIH's increasing difficulties in recruiting top-notch postdoctoral candidates was summarized as follows by another lab chief:

> It's largely an issue of manpower: There are too few American biomedical Ph.D.s available. For basic, fundamental science, there are 20 places as good as NIH in the U.S. This was not so before the glory days of the late 1960s-early 1970s and the "yellow berets" [scientists who joined the Pub-

lic Health Service to avoid being drafted and sent to Vietnam] when NIH had a critical mass of the nation's best young scientists. Ironically, this group went on to seed other research institutions throughout the country, and in succeeding in this mission, they created competition for NIH in attracting the best scientists.

NIH is addressing the manpower shortage issue through mechanisms other than postdoctoral trainees. Another NIH lab chief explained:

The Fogarty Center accounts for only a small part of the presence of foreigners. There are many contractor firms that have many foreigners (such as Russians, Chinese, Indians, Vietnamese, and Arabs) who work on the NIH campus. At the National Library of Medicine (NLM), for example, there are about 1,000 workers. Of these, about 600 are NIH American employees, and about 400 are contract workers, of which about three out of four are foreigners. They specialize in electrical engineering and computer science.

According to several other individuals, the cost issue is also a consideration behind the presence of so many foreign postdocs at NIH. One of these informants, a technician in one of the labs said, "It's money. Foreign scientists have money from their own country. Usually two years are funded by their own country. So foreign labor at NIH is free labor." Not all agreed with the cost argument. From the perspective of one, "cost saving is not an issue. You [can] get good motivation and bad people. Not enough U.S. candidates apply if you have postdoctoral positions to be filled." One problem several lab chiefs reported was how to separate the promising from the not-so-good foreign candidates. One complained that he received a "lot of foreign applications, but you can't check out their references." Another indicated that with the advent of e-mail, matters have gotten worse. Some foreign candidates sent e-mails wholesale to NIH in the hope that any one lab may offer them a postdoctoral appointment. Laboratories often receive hundreds of foreign applications.

Several also noted that foreign postdocs are brought to NIH because of their particular expertise in some areas, such as their skills in quantitative methods. "In our laboratory," one scientist said, "we hire specialties and skill. We don't care if they are foreign born. We look for the best." Many emphasized that foreign scientists are prized for their high motivation and strong work ethic.

The views of former NIH administrators and scientists were particularly revealing because they had intimate knowledge of the inner workings of the institution, some from the managerial perspective, while no longer having turf to defend or an ax to grind regarding current NIH policy. This was especially obvious in the insights several of them provided regarding the surge in the number of foreign biomedical scientists at NIH.

Many noted that one of the purposes of the international postdoctoral training programs run by Fogarty and individual institutes is indeed to forge useful and cooperative relations with foreign scientists and institutions to promote international biomedical research and obtain valuable scientific information from abroad. They also pointed out that NIH offers training fellowships as well as occasional staff positions to foreign scientists because it cannot find enough U.S. scientists qualified in certain specialized disciplines and fields, such as cell biology, neuroscience, computational biology, and several clinical research areas.

Some also claimed that a prominent American political agenda largely explains why since the 1980s the number of foreign postdoctoral trainees at NIH has risen significantly. There are now so many foreign postdocs at NIH, according to a former NIH lab chief currently associated with a leading national research university, in part because of a contraction in the number of full-time positions, or FTE (full-time equivalent) slots, in the institutes. The contraction became threatening beginning in the early 1980s as the administrations of President Reagan and later of President Bush downsized the federal work force, not only at NIH but across the government. Given this situation, NIH looked to Fogarty as an alternative source of scientific labor. It was seen that by emphasizing NIH's role as a training institution, Fogarty postdoctoral fellows could be used at no cost to the institutes' budgets to work in the labs—and the existing job slots could be saved for real, permanent employees. The branch and lab chiefs saw this as a good way to ensure a constant supply of labor.

A retired top administrative NIH official concurred with that view. He described how he had witnessed the Reagan administration's intense effort to reduce the number of civil service jobs through the process of reduction in force (RIF). The administration had a clearly stated bias against public employment and in favor of the private sector, which it considered to be more efficient, effective, and inexpensive. An example of this thrust toward privatization of government functions was Office of Management and Budget (OMB) Circular A76, which required all federal agencies to do one of two things:

1. either prove that their support staff (janitorial, kitchen, etc.) could function more cheaply than people provided by private contractors; or
2. RIF support staff and then contract out support functions.

This created chaos at NIH. It especially affected minorities and women who were highly represented among support personnel—and whom the contractors might offer to hire for one year, but without the benefit packages they had enjoyed as federal employees, and with no assurance of longer employment.

At the professional level, at NIH and everywhere else throughout the federal government, the number of contracted positions mushroomed as the number of federal jobs diminished. Expanding the number of postdoctoral fellows was in keeping with this strategy. A former Fogarty Center official provides still another perspective as to why in a context of less government since the 1980s and into the 1990s, the use of postdoctoral trainees became an ever more attractive option at NIH:

> In the 1980s, NIH had difficulty in attracting Americans because the stipends were too low, especially in light of the fact that most Americans had acquired debts through student loans they had to repay. Foreigners were attracted through Fogarty fellowships. Americans resented the fact that only foreigners could qualify for Fogarty fellowships, especially because foreigners mainly had their education sponsored by their countries' governments, whereas most Americans had paid for all or part of their education and often still owed money. Someone or some group drew attention to this anomalous situation, which caused embarrassment for NIH. In response, NIH established the IRTA program that pays stipends for American fellows that are at least equivalent to Fogarty fellowships.

A former senior administrative official remarked that "if the members of Congress knew about the huge shadow population of thousands of contract scientists that now work at NIH, they would probably have a fit." He explained that today these include scientists of all kinds, including biomedical scientists specializing in genetic research, biomedical engineers, and computer scientists and engineers. The contract firms supply the numbers and types of scientists required by the various institutes and centers at NIH, and these scientists work on campus, often side by side with NIH staff scientists. This individual further pointed out that because each institute and center does its own contracting, it is virtually impossible for anyone to know exactly how many firms and how many individuals are involved and to quantify this phenomenon. But he speculated that the numbers must be significant.

While it is not possible to tell how many foreign scientists are working under contract at NIH, the proportion seems considerable. Indians and Japanese appear to be especially well represented. The contract firms have the capability and expertise to easily take care of visa and immigration issues for foreigners they want to hire, and it is routine for them to make the necessary arrangements. According to one former senior staff member, all of the contract scientists seem to be very well credentialed and to be well paid—Americans and foreigners alike. Because they spend a long time working alongside NIH staff and fellows, they can get to know them well, and they are therefore able to confidently make recommendations about them if their employers indicate that they are intending to hire more scientists and seek suggestions.

Furthermore, another stated that it was the decision of the NIH Director to change policy and to sign letters of no objection (see chapter 5) when J–1 visa holders decided to apply for status adjustment. It was noted that this change would certainly not have been generated by USIA or the Immigration and Naturalization Service (INS), whose mandates are to adhere strictly to legislative intent. And in this case, the entire rationale for the J–1 visa for visiting fellows is to permit foreigners to reside in the United States only temporarily for educational purposes, and then for them to return home and benefit their respective countries by sharing and applying what they have learned in the United States. Indeed, a few years ago there was even talk at the Fogarty Center of asking Congress to establish a special temporary visa category exclusively for NIH to ·help the institutes avoid the political problems and paperwork burden associated with the J–1 and H–1B visa categories.

American trainees currently at NIH presented a combination of reasons as to why they thought NIH seeks foreign scientists. Many of these centered around NIH's desire to be able to draw on the entire world to attract the best-trained and most strongly motivated young scientists and to create an intellectually stimulating and culturally diverse environment for the pursuit of biomedical science. In the words of one American postdoctoral fellow, the objective is

> To fill NIH with the best from around the world and continue its tradition of setting the standard of excellence in scientific research. NIH does not just train research skills, it teaches a set of attitudes. It teaches scientists from around the world that they can work together and benefit from a diverse grouping of scientists.

A number of U.S. trainees also pointed out that most Americans do not want to undertake careers in grueling biomedical research and that other U.S. training institutions compete with NIH for the most talented of the relatively few Americans who do. Further, they observed, the chance to spend time at NIH represents for many young foreign scientists a great opportunity not available to them in their home countries. Thus, NIH casts abroad

> In order to tap a larger talent pool. NIH is looking for the brightest individuals who are willing to spend much time and effort without obvious reward—that would mean the foreign born, especially from more disadvantaged countries.

As another noted,

> Americans are not willing to work long hours, to sacrifice, for science; but foreigners, especially East Asians, are willing to do intensive labor. Americans want MBAs or law degrees. The same situation is true at universities as at NIH: There are not enough U.S. [science] Ph.D.s.

Some speculated as to whether NIH brings in these foreigners for training—or instead to serve as needed professional manpower in the guise of trainees. One person clearly thought the latter to be the case:

> Foreigners enter NIH postdocs with an incredible skill level. They don't need any more training. They are doing their postdoc here for the connection building. Basically, for many foreign postdocs, NIH is a finishing school. And the result is foreigners are creating the norm. NIH is no longer training or teaching, which is assumed to be the main goal of a postdoctorate education.

Yet others saw the situation as being more complicated because of the multi-faceted role of NIH:

> I think it makes NIH more competitive. But I do not think this is the only reason or the main reason why NIH hires foreign scientists. I think NIH has to do a balancing act. It is trying to produce excellent research but ethically it has a responsibility to facilitate good research throughout the world. NIH is pulled by the government and international competition in science, but as a scientific organization, it believes in open communication and research collaboration.

One individual stressed the importance of the professional, personal, and ethnic "pipelines" that are maintained by NIH lab chiefs with their counterparts in foreign institutions that serve as conduits for foreign trainees to NIH. He estimated that as many as half of the foreigners at NIH found their way there through these established channels.

U.S. scientists who had formerly received training at NIH identified lack of interest among Americans in the pursuit of careers in biomedical research, and hence the lack of available American trainees, as the key reason why NIH brings in scientists from abroad. In the view of one, NIH does so

> To make the pool of applicants larger. Interest in science [in the United States] has diminished in the last 30 years. Also, [American] people are more materialistic today. Therefore, the NIH must look to other countries.

Some emphasized NIH's mandate to expand the frontiers of biomedical knowledge and health through international cooperation. Thus, NIH seeks

> To obtain the best and brightest from throughout the world—to not have limits on the scientific talent that is drawn from the best institutions around the world (in such countries such as Sweden, Great Britain, Japan, Italy, and Germany). And these scientists then return to these institutions. This has created ongoing cooperation, a kind of Marshall Plan for science, for distributing knowledge around the world. If NIH wanted to advertise highly, it could probably fill all of the training positions with Americans, but it obviously wants foreigners. The foreign trainees are selected very carefully by the lab chiefs, who know the institutions they are coming from and often personally know their mentors. (At NIH, the lab chiefs are the king[s] of the hill: everybody above services them, and everybody below works for them.) The lab chiefs treat the foreigners very well, with re-

spect, and make sure that they have a good experience here, and in this way they foster good relations with the foreign institutions.

Others saw a combination of factors to be in play. One person stated that NIH's principal objective in bringing in foreign scientists is to obtain "cheap labor." However, he added,

> This movement of foreign scientists also promotes the exchange of scientific knowledge between countries. Also, it helps foreign countries to bootstrap up their abilities when their scientists return home with new knowledge and skills.

And another said,

> But I think even more than forging international connections, the fact that foreign students are more dedicated than Americans is the major reason NIH hires more foreign students.

Many foreign trainees at NIH felt that they are offered postdoctoral training opportunities primarily because there is a shortage of young American biomedical scientists. The general line of thinking assumes that the benefits of pursuing a scientific career in the United States are not in line with the rewards, especially monetary, that graduates can expect in relation to lifetime earning streams in other fields, such as business, law, and medicine. Financial rewards in these occupations are much higher in relation to the amount of time and effort devoted to achieving a higher education degree. A naturalized Canadian of Chinese origin expressed this view when he stated, "There is not much money in scientific research and most Americans place a high priority on making 'easy money.' Therefore, many talented Americans who could be scientists choose not to, this being the reason why NIH has places for foreigners." A corollary of this reasoning is that NIH invites foreign scientists because U.S. scientists are unwilling to come to NIH and work for the available stipend. NIH is forced to rely on foreign postdoctoral trainees since it cannot compete with other industries in terms of salary. Foreign scientists "cost less and work harder." Thus, NIH flourishes by depending on foreign postdocs who fill vacant positions. Only one foreign postdoc, a French experimental bioimmunologist, categorically departed from this position when he observed that "NIH does not need to look to foreign scientists to fill research positions."

A few NIH foreign trainees have concluded, on the other hand, that foreign biomedical scientists are given the opportunity to pursue postdoctoral training at NIH primarily because the United States is unable to educate enough American biomedical scientists. The demand is huge and no single country can train so many top-level scientists. In addition, NIH wants the best and the brightest the world has to offer. A Russian molecular biologist summarized this perspective:

> NIH is always looking for the best talent available anywhere in the world. Whenever they can identify scientists with the skills they are looking for, the scientists express an interest in coming to NIH, and, if NIH has the resources to do so, foreign scientists are hired. However, this hiring occurs on a short-term basis; it is extremely difficult for a foreign scientist to receive a permanent job at NIH.

Postdoctoral foreign trainees do not universally share this exalted view of NIH. According to the experiences of a German pharmaceutical chemist, "NIH does not hire the best and the brightest, because I am not working with the best and the brightest. AIDS research at NIH can attract the best and brightest because the work here is fascinating in that field, but in my field it is not as interesting."

Many of the foreign postdoctoral scientists thought that their presence in the United States is determined by NIH's cultural exchange objective, including the promotion of cross-national research. They held that it is for this reason that NIH has its own international exchange division. The United States gives as much as it receives by training foreign scientists in that many of them have the potential to or actually make outstanding contributions to biomedical research. NIH is also interested in having the different ideas and perspectives that can only be accessed through a diversity of cultures. America remains abreast of basic science developments in other countries and also about biotechnology research trends. "By dipping into a larger pool of trained people," one Australian biochemist commented, "NIH has more choice."

Some foreign scientists asserted that the way NIH selects its postdoctoral trainees undermines the cultural diversity objective. A Chinese biochemist complained, for instance, that "NIH could have done a better job. People concentrate in labs with a principal investigator from the same country. The macro-environment is diverse—most of the postdocs are Visiting Fellows—but the micro environment of individual labs is not." A comparable assessment was made by another scientist who noted that "at the National Cancer Institute, [postdocs] are mostly foreigners from Eastern Europe. NCI hires a lot of Russians because the faculty members [sic] have connections with Russia." These revelations are indicative of the relative isolation many foreign postdocs feel at NIH and of the power of social co-ethnic networks in migration, even at the highest levels of educational attainment.

The presence of large numbers of foreign postdoctoral trainees at NIH, according to an Indian biochemist, is also logical given the greater knowledge American postdocs have about the politics of which labs and institutions are likely to do most to advance their careers. Highly qualified Americans are more selective than foreign scientists regarding where they pursue postdoctoral training, such as at top-ranked educational institutions.

Several foreign postdocs noted that NIH likes foreign postdoctoral trainees, as mentioned by an Israeli molecular biologist, because they are easier to control due to their temporary tenure and visa status. In general, foreign scientists are regarded as less expensive, more malleable, willing to work longer hours, and not as demanding as Americans. As a Chinese scientist who graduated with a molecular biology doctoral degree from a leading British university stated, "lots of Americans don't want to do the work—the hard work—of research. My lab has mostly Mainland Chinese foreign fellows, which the lab directors seem to like because 'Chinese don't complain.'" Several commented that foreign scientists work harder with the hope of being noted and finding an institution willing to sponsor them for the green card.

Foreign scientists pointed out that many of them come to NIH (and more generally to the United States) because of the research opportunities and the money. For people in poorer countries, even the limited stipends by U.S. standards offered by NIH are far more generous than what they can earn at home. Also, in biotechnology there are not really very many other options. "The other leading biotechnology country is Japan, but I could not go there because it would be such a different culture," reasoned a French virologist linked to the Pasteur Institute. Further, as a Czech Republic cell biologist pointed out, scientists are willing to spend a lot of time working in the lab because they see NIH as a great opportunity. "These people work harder than Americans. They focus only on their work. They come because of the good reputation of NIH. It's good for finding work later." Despite some frustrations, the gains arising from a stint at NIH are perceived as real. A German molecular biologist came expecting to have contact with well-known scientists. She was frustrated when she realized that it does not happen often: "Scientific luminaries," she noted, "stay in their offices and you never see them." Nonetheless, she felt that overall the NIH experience has been good for her.

While the economic motivations of scientists from developing countries could be anticipated, such considerations were also very important to Western European postdoctoral trainees. The number of European biomedical trainees at NIH is significant and on the increase. According to an informal survey of 203 NIH European postdocs (including, among others, German, British, Spanish, and French trainees) conducted by a French trainee who provided us access to the results, 90 percent claimed to have come to NIH seeking further scientific training. When asked if they were planning to return to Europe, an equal percentage indicated they were not certain, alleging that they were worried about career prospects back home.

A public forum sponsored by the European Community Research Organization—a foreign trainee interest group—at the NIH campus, attended by approximately 200 European postdocs, and observed by a member of the research team, provided an opportunity for trainees to vent their career concerns with representatives from the European Union. Many voiced displeasure with the small number of research grants available in Europe to biomedical scientists. They asserted that funding was too limited and, when available, mostly targeted to achieve specific applied outcomes.

The impression gained of the meeting was that it was convened by a European Union worried about a growing tendency among its scientists to remain in the United States. One purpose was to convince more of them to go back to Europe once their training appointments ended by conveying the policy measures being weighed to make the return more attractive. Some of the European Union policy initiatives included establishing more postdoctoral opportunities in Europe; encouraging European universities to work more closely with industry, as American higher education institutions do; and strengthening international research linkages to take advantage of the growing globalization trend. It was also suggested that European postdocs return and establish their own start-up biotechnology companies. Most postdocs left the meeting expressing the feeling that not much was being changed. Their comments suggested that even among Western European postdoctoral trainees, the motivations to come to the United States, and to perhaps eventually settle here, may be as potent as they are for scientists from developing countries.

Former NIH postdoctoral foreign trainees that had returned to their home countries provided several complementary explanations to account for why NIH offers fellowships to international scientists. Among these were NIH's desire to comply with its stated mission to forge international links with the world-wide biomedical scientific community; to identify, get to know, and, when justified, recruit some of the most promising young biomedical scientists in the world; to reduce the costs of conducting research by bringing to NIH foreign scientists willing to work harder and for less compensation than Americans; and to respond to biomedical labor supply and demand considerations.

A typical explanation emphasizing NIH's international biomedical mission was provided by an Argentinean physician:

> Several factors account for the presence of foreign researchers. It is an international center of excellence for biomedical research given its ample resources and scholarships. It offers foreign scientists a unique and valuable research experience. The U.S. federal government has endless resources that it uses to bring together know-how from the world over to obtain the raw material to develop the most advanced health knowledge.

Many of the returned foreign scientists referred to NIH and its international education mission in glowing terms. During the interview, for example, one person repeatedly interjected, "I love NIH, and I love the United States." While most were not as exuberant as this, they also described NIH as both the largest scientific enterprise and the most important center for biomedical training in the world. "NIH brings together the best from many countries, trains them, and helps develop close personal and professional links among them." NIH is "sort of a biomedical United Nations." One lamented, "I wish Argentina had a place to bring together so many ideas and points of view."

A number of the foreign scientists noted that the fellowships provided by NIH are relatively easy to obtain and do not require going through too much bureaucratic paperwork. Further, according to another, for historical reasons NIH must accept foreign postdocs since

American scientists were at first restricted in their eligibility for the fellowships because the Fogarty program was specifically designed for foreign scientists. Thus, NIH was and continues to be obliged to recruit abroad. At the same time, "since NIH is the emporium of biomedical sciences, young researchers worldwide dream of spending some time there." Nowhere else in the world, it was pointed out, can a researcher find all that NIH has to offer, from bibliographical resources, specialized courses, English classes for foreigners, and a chance to publish, all in exchange for a young scientist's willingness to work very hard for a few years.

Some former foreign trainees believed that while the foreign training programs undoubtedly have considerable scientific merit and are designing to promote international cooperation, the United States also funds them for self-serving and not totally disinterested reasons. One perspective suggests that NIH likes foreign investigators because they come when they are most productive (between thirty and forty years of age), the ages at which they mature scientifically and are totally devoted to research. NIH can also draw from a large pool of already well-trained research scientists. An agenda behind the foreign fellowships may be, according to an Australian biochemist, "that foreign scientists work very hard," in part because by "being out of their usual cultural milieu and life styles, many of them concentrate on productive work in a minimum amount of time."

Foreign postdocs may also be offered training positions, according to some interviewees, as a way to lower research costs and permanently recruit talented foreign researchers. A former fellow, now a research biologist in Argentina, claimed that the main reason driving the employment of foreign scientists is cost. He perceived foreign scientists as a source of cheap labor: "If all NIH investigators were Americans, costs will at least triple." In the words of another, foreign researchers provide NIH with "scientific infantry." One person noted that thanks to the presence of so many foreign postdocs, NIH can draw from a large pool of already well-trained scientists. And the foreign scientists are well aware that "labor mobility between both groups of scientists [postdocs and permanent NIH research staff] is continuous and that long-term opportunities are available for foreign scientists." This statement suggests that foreign postdocs recognize that they are eligible, in principle, for the fiercely competitive career-track appointments at NIH, even if under highly unfavorable odds.

Some interviewees took issue with the notion that foreign scientists are provided with fellowships as a means to access cheap labor; what they saw instead is a symbiotic relationship. Most foreign scientists earn more at NIH than in any other country (whether developed or developing), and in return they give much of themselves because they encounter ideal working conditions. As one described it, "At NIH they are not particularly interested in foreign scientists; it is the foreign scientists who want to go to NIH."

Further, some foreign scientists commented that much is expected from postdoctoral researchers in general, and more particularly from those who wish to be asked to become permanent NIH research staff. As a result, the research endeavor at NIH is "prodigious"; if all staff were Americans, it would be far different. One asserted that there is a normal distribution of intelligence worldwide (not the patrimony of any country); by having NIH, the United States can manage to capture the most brilliant foreign biomedical scientists. Work conditions at NIH are "ideal." Through a filtering process, NIH eventually gets to keep many top foreign investigators while not interfering with the research goals of U.S. scientists. This individual noted that while institutional objectives at NIH may change over time, one thing remains constant: "having foreign researchers."

Finally, foreign scientists are offered training positions, according to many of the former fellows who returned to their countries, simply because this is one of the ways in which NIH addresses scientific talent supply and demand considerations. From this perspective, foreign scientists go to NIH because relatively few Americans are interested in research or in the low salaries biomedical scientists earn. There is a shortage of young American scientists to satisfy postdoctoral trainee demand. In addition, American scientists shun NIH because they earn more money working for industry and because NIH does not offer training on how to obtain grants, a requirement for employment at many universities.

Former foreign NIH postdoctoral trainees who remained in the United States believed that NIH provides training opportunities to foreign scientists primarily for two reasons. The first is that NIH wants to comply with its mandate to establish international scientific linkages and promote cultural exchange programs. Some felt exchange programs to some extent also reflect United States foreign policies, as Washington is intent both in showcasing its generosity and in helping the country maintain its international dominance in the biomedical field. Several foreign scientists noted, however, that NIH could do a much better job of promoting cultural exchange and diversity. Far too often foreign scientists concentrate in labs headed by natives of their own countries. In the lab where a Polish-born scientist worked while he was at NIH, for example, there were no Americans, with most postdoctoral trainees being from Japan and Eastern Europe.

Many of the foreign postdocs remaining in the United States were of the opinion that foreign scientists are invited to come to NIH because the institution needs them. There are several variants to this theme, but most of them rest on the assumption that foreign scientists have much to contribute to scientific research. Some claimed that deficiencies in the American educational system have created a dearth of well-trained biomedical scientists, while others believed that NIH benefits from the presence of foreign postdoctoral trainees since they are very well educated, hard working, and "easier to control." An argument made by many of these scientists was that since the number of applicants from all parts of the world by far exceeds the number of available slots, NIH reaps major benefits by selecting the cream of the world crop of young biomedical scientists. An extension of this argument was that NIH—and the United States generally—has no other choice given that in recent years the quality of American education has declined dramatically and there are not enough natives qualified for the demanding tasks of biomedical research. They reasoned that few American students are well trained in the sciences and most lack the discipline to pursue demanding studies; even fewer are willing to make the sacrifices needed to complete a Ph.D. A permanent U.S. resident of Russian origin currently employed at NIH provided an extreme example of this view when he stated:

> I graduated from the best high school in Russia and it was much harder than Harvard . . . American education is student driven. Students pick their courses and therefore [in the United States] miss out on much needed good baseline knowledge. When I lectured at a college, I realized that students did not have knowledge of basic scientific principles.

Another view is that foreign scientists are offered NIH postdoctoral positions simply because the stipends offered by NIH are too low compared to what is available to American scientists at other institu-

Summary

In sum, current and former NIH administrators and scientists, and current and former American and foreign postdocs in the United States and abroad, provided these explanations as to why foreign biomedical scientists come to NIH and to the United States more generally:

- NIH offers training opportunities to foreign scientists in fulfilling its mandate to create international biomedical research linkages.
- An important complementary reason is to fill the demand gap left by the limited number of people in the United States willing to pursue the rigorous academic training demanded by these disciplines. This was largely explained by the availability of other better-paid and less demanding career options in fields such as law, medicine, and business.

As a result, U.S. training and research institutions such as NIH must supplement the pool of available U.S. scientists by offering temporary training opportunities or permanent employment positions to foreign scientists. At the same time, foreign scientists flock to NIH and other U.S. training institutions lured by the chance to further their knowledge in unparalleled American research institutions.

- Despite government directives to reduce federal manpower levels, NIH has been able to maintain sufficient staffing to effectively utilize the considerable congressional funding increases for biomedical research made during the last two decades.

NIH had two options. One was to expand the number of training slots for foreign as well as for U.S. postdocs, and the other was to indirectly employ domestic and foreign scientists as contract workers. Both options were implemented.

- Many scientists, particularly the foreign born, felt that NIH realizes significant monetary savings by relying on foreign trainees.

This view was prevalent among the foreign scientists who returned to their home countries as well as among those who stayed in the United States.

Finally, and regardless of NIH motivations, there was a universal perception that foreign biomedical scientists seek training fellowships

at NIH and in other American institutions for two main, often complementary, reasons:

- Many of those applying for NIH fellowships from countries like mainland China and India do so as part of a long-term personal economic
  improvement strategy in which emigration plays an important part.
- For many others, including those from economically advanced European countries and Japan, the principal magnet is the leadership of the
  United States in biomedical and biotechnology research, together with
  superior and more abundant training opportunities.

Comparisons of Foreign and American Biomedical Scientists and Trainees at NIH

Training, Motivation, Skills and Performance

Most current NIH administrators and scientists claimed that, on
average, foreign and U.S. biomedical scientists are equivalent in terms
of training, motivation, skills, and performance. At the level of training required for scientists at NIH, they asserted, differences are not
very substantial since scientists from abroad are drawn from the world's
intellectual elite. Some noted, nonetheless, that foreign scientists in
some instances differ in some dimensions as a function of the world
regions in which they were trained. According to one scientist,

> Western Europeans are well trained and competitive—at least as good as
> Americans. Scientists from the former Soviet Union and the newly inde-
> pendent states of Eastern Europe have strong bases in physical sciences.
> Third world scientists lack knowledge due to lack of resources, but they
> rapidly adapt.

American and European scientists were said to challenge authority
more, whereas Asians were typified by hard work and respect for
authority. One interviewee, a foreign-born senior staff fellow, summarized his observations about foreign postdocs by saying, "Those from
China, India, and Japan are very good in basic math and science
compared to those from the U.S. Americans have broader knowledge,
especially of applications. The U.S. scientists have more broad knowledge because they have had choices in academic courses that scientists
from other countries do not."

Another remarked that the only difference he saw was "in the social interaction in the lab. Foreigners are more introverted and for them communication is a barrier." One NIH scientist said that "foreign scientists are better motivated and work harder because their general training is poorer and their technical training background is lower than [for their] U.S. counterparts," but another took issue with this assessment by pointing out that not all foreign scientists "have high motivation." Often they tend to work harder "because they don't have family responsibilities." That which foreign scientists lack in applied laboratory skills, another interviewee asserted, they more than make up in adaptability: "They catch up very fast to meet the American laboratory standards of performance."

According to one former NIH administrator, the differences between domestic and foreign postdocs are not very significant due to the manner in which foreign fellowship applicants are chosen. The number of foreign applicants far exceeds the number of fellowship slots. Branch and lab chiefs (these are essentially the same in terms of functions and rank, the difference being that lab refers to working in wet labs), are good at winnowing out, at selecting for what they want among the foreign postdocs, such as choosing those who have had training in the United States and therefore are more of a known quantity. They are also familiar with which universities abroad produce highly qualified graduates and depend on referrals from foreign scientists whom they respect.

One former senior staff member noted that in terms of overall skills, European scientists are comparable to Americans. They share common knowledge with Americans and have comfort in moving from European to American laboratories. The major differences are with scientists from Asia in terms of education and approaches. They bring these differences to NIH, and this is good for NIH. Another scientist offered a much harsher assessment of the relative skills of foreign scientists. In her view, due to cultural differences, they are much harder to deal with than Americans, and have limited skills regarding the use of state-of-the-art laboratory equipment.

Current NIH American trainees were uniformly complimentary toward their foreign counterparts when comparing training, skills, motivation, and work habits. They described foreign postdocs as possessing training as good as that of U.S. scientists and said that NIH chooses them from among the best that come to its attention. The foreign postdocs were generally viewed as extremely motivated and hard working. One American trainee stated that "we benefit by working with them. I have been taught several practical things by them that we are not usually familiar with."

Here are two examples of favorable comments:

NCI has an incredible diverse background. Foreigners usually come with hard core scientific and technological skills, unlike Americans who often enter their postdoctorate with academic training and no hands on technical skills . . . the foreigners come with hard science (computer skills, physics, mathematics) while the Americans tend to major in something more general like evolutionary biology.

The foreigners are more motivated. They must work harder due to language and cultural barriers.

However, it was also noted that cultural factors can work to the disadvantage of the foreign trainees:

They have the same skills. But I think it is more difficult for foreigners to adapt to the culture of NIH. The two big problems for foreign scientists are: (1) they feel opportunities to stay are limited, and there are no easy transitions to go from a visiting scientist to a permanent resident working in America; and (2) foreigners need to adapt to both the culture of the United States and the culture of NIH. The culture of NIH is that the clock is constantly ticking. A scientist needs to be productive. And the proof of productivity is publishing and attending seminars. Scientists need to be able to see the wide view of how to transition from NIH into a career. They need to know how to network. Foreigners are at a disadvantage when their basic command of English needs work. They will not be as well informed as an American on how to tailor their c.v. for a particular job in industry or academia. I consider these pitfalls to come under the rubric of culture. This is the area where the mentor needs to really need foreigners. Because if they do not it becomes easy for foreigners to feel like they are just fodder for the cannon—cheap labor. With a good mentor, foreigners have opportunities.

A couple of people observed distinctions between foreign and U.S. scientists in regard to the conduct of clinical research. One remarked,

In this institute, there is lots of clinical work (such as clinical trials), which most often means U.S. citizens or U.S.-trained because the P.I.s [principal investigators] are surer of U.S. medical training than of foreign medical training.

Also, some commented on variance in workplace interactions. For example,

U.S. fellows may have more collegial relations with senior investigators, but there are confounding variables (for example, at this time in this lab, only Americans are senior fellows, who are more likely to have collegial relations with senior staff than are junior fellows). Asians are more deferential toward senior staff.

Former NIH American trainees generally felt that foreign scientists were comparable to them in terms of technical training and skills. A number commented admiringly on the strong early education of foreign trainees, and especially on the high motivation and dedicated work habits of Asian scientists:

The education and training for foreign scientists is superior to American training in high school and undergraduate.

The Asians work longer hours and are more experienced, because of their [early] education. I think ethnicity plays a big role as far as culturally learned characteristics of motivation. I think foreign scientists come to work with a more single-minded focus than Americans do.

It was often noted by former postdoctoral American trainees that working conditions at NIH are far from comfortable and leisurely, and that people from different backgrounds vary in how well they adapt. The next two statements illustrate this point:

The lab chiefs want a bunch of coolies; they want to do the creative work themselves. Everybody has to work very hard. It is very demanding. In other places, limitations on money limit the amount of work that can be done, but at NIH there is no limit on money, only on time, and everybody is expected to work after hours and on weekends, which isn't true elsewhere. The Europeans have a little more trouble with the pace and pressure. The Japanese help each other out a lot.

At NIH the conditions are pretty bad for everyone. The major differences in my lab were that people from different countries (especially China and Japan) were put together by the lab chief in different rooms. At first I thought this might indicate some kind of discrimination, but after a while I saw its benefits. In this way, people from the same countries—like China and Japan—could communicate and cooperate better (which is more their style of work) on a daily working basis and deal with the principal investigators and lab chief through their own spokesmen.

It was pointed out that language differences at times pose difficulties among researchers at NIH, but that these do not tend to be of marked importance. One individual stated that "the communication barrier at times is a problem, but not so much that it prevents foreign scientists from performing some functions." Another made this interesting observation:

Sometimes there was difficulty communicating due to the language barrier, but not usually. Actually, the biggest factor that determined delegation of work was gender. The women were expected to answer the phone when it rang in the lab and take notes.

No other significant differences were noted between foreigners and Americans in regard to roles or division of labor.

In regard to skills, many current NIH foreign trainees regarded foreigners and Americans as equal, except for the language barrier. Foreigners must work harder to compensate for the language handicap. According to one foreign postdoc, most foreign scientists at NIH are more experienced than American scientists who often have just finished their doctoral level studies. However, he felt that many foreign scientists lack English communication skill, which makes it difficult for them to compete on an even keel with U.S. scientists.

Other than language, there appeared to be cultural factors that help account for some of the perceived differences in attitudes. Some foreign scientists, East Asians (Chinese, Koreans, Japanese) and South Asians (Indians, Pakistanis) in particular, were described by many informants, irrespective of nationality, as more focused, disciplined, team oriented, hard working, and generally as having a stronger work ethic. Self-descriptions of foreign postdoctoral trainees attitudes often coincided with one another in that many of them saw themselves as working harder than Americans by focusing their lives almost exclusively on their work. Some were less categorical when they observed, as one did, that "it is hard to say, in a macro-level, whether U.S. scientists or foreign scientists are more intelligent or smarter. Many U.S. scientists here work very hard, and often work overtime." In general, Japanese regarded themselves as harder working, more organized and efficient, and as having better skills for experiments than Americans. One Japanese scientist also noted that "we don't like messy things; we like to keep our labs and homes very clean." He regarded Americans as more interactive and dynamic. Knowledge-wise, however, he saw no differences.

Several foreign trainees parted company with the cultural argument and tend to describe differences primarily in terms of type of training. A French postdoc provided one example when he said: "I think the people are the same; I think the training is different. To land a postdoctoral position you need to be specialized. I did my Ph.D. in pharmacy, so I was less specialized than most foreigners, but I was still more specialized than most Americans."

Another frequent observation was that except for Europeans and some Asians, the training background of foreign fellows is not as good as that provided in the United States because facilities in other countries are inadequate. Further, one scientist commented that although foreign and U.S. scientists have the same intelligence and knowledge, scientists from poorer countries often have not acquired basic bench research skills. Whereas foreign scientists are more knowledgeable of basic systemic science, U.S. scientists are better at chemistry, more focused and technical.

Most current NIH foreign postdocs, however, felt that differences in training, knowledge, and skills between foreign and U.S. scientists are minimal. As one expressed it: "everyone working at NIH is a smart guy, and every one has his own strong points or weakness, whether American or foreign." Perceived differences in theoretical knowledge between foreign and American trainees were explained by some in terms of diverse educational traditions in the following terms:

> In Germany, at the undergraduate level, you have to choose what you want to get a degree in and most of your classes are in this field. And if you want to get your masters in a different degree area you have to repeat you undergraduate degree in that new area of interest. This is very different from the American education system which stresses liberal arts and if you get your undergraduate degree in chemistry and then decide to switch to physics you still have a good chance of getting into the physics program if

your GREs [Graduate Record Examination] are high enough. This leads to the Americans being less trained and less specialized than the foreigners. Another disadvantage of the American education system is the fact that the rich tend to get into the best universities in the United States and obviously, just because they are rich, does not mean they are the most skilled or intelligent. These disadvantages of U.S. education need to change.

A striking pattern emerged from many of the interviews with current foreign NIH postdoctoral trainees. Several indicated that they could not discuss with any certainty whether or not there were differences between U.S. and foreign scientists primarily because, as one of them said, "I have never worked with a U.S. scientist at NIH; even my boss is from another country." A not too atypical response during interviews was: "I don't know how accurate my perceptions are. I don't know a lot of American scientists because there aren't many American scientists; [there is only] one American out of ten postdocs in my lab."

More often than not, former NIH foreign trainees interviewed abroad offered cautious and balanced assessments when comparing the skills and motivations of foreign and U.S. scientists. Some expressed misgivings about making comparisons in part because the mix of foreign and American scientists varies from lab to lab, although, as a general rule, foreign scientists predominate in most. Echoing the observations made by current foreign trainees, some of the former ones interviewed in their home countries also commented that they were hard pressed to compare American and foreign scientists because while they were at NIH, there were too few of the former in the labs to which they had been assigned. They also cautioned that work environments varied from lab to lab, a factor which may impinge on judgments made by different individuals. It was pointed out that research areas should be considered as well, since some are more competitive than others, while some are fashionable and others are not. Also, cultural differences manifest themselves more in the way tasks are approached than in results.

One significant difference reported by several of the interviewees was that the American approach to research is pragmatic and emphasized method over theory. A female Argentinean physician marveled at how American scientists carry the theoretical to the practical, described the American research approach as very different from what she knew, and confessed to being very pleased to have learned to work as Americans do. In contrast, an Australian biochemist claimed that American postdoctoral trainees lack commitment to their work. He charged that "Americans are not hard working, nor do they care about obtaining good results in experiments." He compared that attitude with that of foreigners who are very dedicated and feel they must give the best they have. However, this individual did not perceive any differences between American and foreign scientists in terms of intelligence or qualifications.

Some former foreign trainees interviewed abroad, although not all, believed that cultural differences are not related to work output. What really counts is the type of training received and that this needs to be assessed from a multicultural perspective. In this connection, one scientist reported that in general U.S. and foreign investigators differ in work habits and objectives. He felt that Americans, like the Japanese, are very pragmatic and not as theory oriented as Europeans and Latin Americans. Americans and Japanese both place great emphasis on methods and on the management of research. Their research is guided by specific objectives, work is organized according to those objectives, and leads to good results. In contrast, Chinese scientists were said to be weak, for example, in terms of experimental performance and scientific rigor, as are scientists of several other nationalities. On the other hand, some stressed that creativity has nothing to do with nationality or culture, but rather with individual personalities and experiences.

Asian scientists were often described by former postdoctoral trainees as prone to put aside everything else in their lives to perform well at work. They distinguish themselves for the long hours and the intensity they put into work. Asian researchers, Chinese in particular, were seen as not very creative, but as quick to learn and master new techniques.

Some differences in research skills were reported between scientists with Ph.D.s and those without them [those with M.D.s exclusively], with experimental skills being particularly more limited among foreign-trained physicians. It was claimed that many physicians do not have Ph.D.s, are poorly trained in statistics, and cannot test hypotheses.

According to a German interviewee, some of the foreign postdocs could benefit from training in modern biomedical research techniques. He felt, however, that in terms of performance "foreigners are more likely to do better than average since they are under more intense pressure to succeed."

One physician commented that a winnowing-out process is at work at NIH that tends to minimize differences among NIH postdoctoral trainees, and that most are well qualified. "In my lab," he related, "there was a very high percentage of foreign scientists from at least ten countries. Those who are incompetent are let go whether they are Chinese or American . . . At NIH there are really no major national differences in human resources. They all work very hard and they all want to publish."

According to one of the foreign postdocs, the main advantage of Americans is that as a group they have received better and more homogeneous training. For them NIH is not as competitive as, say, the Massachusetts Institute of Technology, which they therefore find more attractive. The differences between American and some of the foreign scientists were described in rather stark terms by one interviewee: Among the postdocs, "foreign scientists go to NIH to be trained, whereas the Americans are already trained." This was felt not to be the case among permanent staff, regardless of where they came from.

Most of the former NIH foreign trainees who had remained in the United States stated that at the level of training achieved by biomedical doctorates, there are no significant differences in skills between foreign and American scientists. Whatever differences may be reported, they are likely to be due to personality and cultural differences. A fairly common view was that foreign scientists at NIH have a stronger work ethic, especially those of Asian background, and they are more hard working and work longer hours than the typical American postdoctoral trainee. Some interviewees explained the foreign scientists' work habits in terms of the desire to remain in the United States. By succeeding in the lab, they hope to attract attention and be offered a permanent position, whether in a university or in industry, and hence gain the opportunity to remain in the United States. The work habits of the foreign scientists, several remarked, is in part driven by their desire to overcome language limitations and by the fact that they do not have much of a social life.

A few of these individuals claimed that Americans scientists have a better mastery of scientific techniques, whereas foreign scientists lag behind in this area when they first arrive, but are better grounded in theory and have superior skills in math and physics. This difference is said to reflect the fact that U.S. science is more intense, better organized, and more results oriented, with American scientists thus usually having a more narrow focus and being more specialized. U.S. scientists were also said to do well in terms of interpersonal and communication skills.

Disciplines and Specialty Areas

In general, current NIH administrators and biomedical scientists reported relatively few differences in specialty areas between U.S. and foreign scientists. Whatever differences were noted were attributed to educational systems and individual abilities. One interviewee indicated, nevertheless, that "U.S. fellows are better at biophysics, biochemistry, and math," and that the United States has "always had an edge in molecular biology, pharmaceutical biology, and biomedical fields."

Some very interesting comments were advanced regarding scientists' differences by nationality. A naturalized, European-born section chief, noted, for instance, that "Japanese scientists [are] more concerned with details and generally more careful in their approach. Italian scientists are usually very creative and daring in exploring new ideas. American young scientists are much more concerned about working on the trend of the moment because this controls their future career and employment opportunities." The description provided by one scientist is consistent with the notion of differences in approaches to research science between foreign and U.S. scientists. This lab chief, who possessed almost a quarter-century of experience at NIH, said that Americans want to do "the cool stuff," cutting-edge work, such as genetics, but not basic science. You cannot get them," he went on, "to do classic stuff such as biochemistry, physiology, and protein chemistry. They have hybrid training and are 'chimeras.' However, they tend to be more innovative."

The perceptions of former NIH administrators and scientists were very similar. All tended to confirm that there are not overwhelming contrasts in terms of the distribution of foreign versus domestic scientists by specialty area, other than a tendency for foreign scientists to be over-represented in new and rapidly growing areas (e.g., computational biology). Some notable differences, however, seemed to be associated with regard to attitude and disposition. One former lab chief described U.S. postdocs as usually capable of showing more flexibility. Also, American postdocs were usually selected over foreigners for clinical fellowships because of their U.S. medical training and licensure. Those from Asia—especially China and Japan—were claimed to have a strong work ethic. They work late, and they are seen to be more malleable. They do the technical work while the lab chief gives guidance.

Most current NIH foreign trainees did not perceive any major differences in disciplines and specialty areas between them and U.S. scientists at NIH. One Asian postdoc indicated, for example, that "in almost every discipline and specialty area you can see United States and foreign scientists working together," while another noted that "within the same level, there is not any obvious difference." Still another postdoctoral trainee observed that not many differences ought to be anticipated since so many of the foreign Fogarty fellows have been trained at American educational institutions. The United States, according to another, has a longer tradition in modern medicine and biology; therefore, American scientists are better in these fields. Although there are isolated instances where greater excellence or advances have been achieved in Japan and Europe, this particular scientist felt that the United States and U.S. scientists in general are best overall in both basic and applied science.

A few other foreign trainees felt that foreign scientists might be better grounded on theory than Americans, although they lack the hands-on experience in which U.S. scientists excel. Another one noted that an important difference is related to biotechnology know-how because many foreign scientists like to train in the United States since in their home countries they seldom have the opportunity to acquire the tools of this industry. In contrast, a Chinese cytologist concluded that foreign and U.S. scientists specialize in different areas. This explained, in his mind, "why sometimes you don't see any U.S. scientists in [some] labs."

It was pointed out by a French postdoc that in some fields, such as computational biology, it appears that foreign scientists have come to dominate. This is an area where there is a preponderance of foreign scientists since they have found a specialized niche given their strong mathematical backgrounds, especially those from the former Soviet Union. But, over the long term, she suggested, the absorption capacity in this narrow field should diminish because demand is not great and saturation comes fast. However, with short-term demand being as high as it is, funding now is readily available.

A Ukrainian molecular biologist believed that foreign scientists occupy the majority of postdoctoral molecular biology and chemistry slots at NIH, and he was virtually certain that they outnumber American scientists in practically every other research specialty. A German biologist added his own ethnographic observation about NIH and American society by pointing out "that of the American scientists, the majority are Jewish. They, as a group, tend to value education much more than your average American. Then you see a sprinkling of Euro-descent Americans and very few Afro-Americans, and no [U.S.] Latin Americans."

Few differences were reported in terms of disciplines and specialty areas among U.S. and foreign trainees by former NIH foreign trainees in their home countries. It was frequently noted that U.S. researchers tend to specialize more in narrow areas and that foreign postdocs tend to be under-represented in clinical areas due to their lack of American professional licensure.

By and large, former NIH foreign trainees who remained in the United States were not cognizant of major differences in the disciplines and specialty areas of foreign and American biomedical scientists. The only notable observation, made by several individuals, was that foreign-educated scientists have better training in basic sciences. This was perceived as being partly driven by language barriers: when you are not proficient in a foreign language, you can always shift to the language of mathematics and science. This may help explain why so many foreign scientists working in the biomedical field can be found in computational biology, a field that has been booming over the last several years due to funding for the Human Genome Project and other developments.

Functions

Almost without exception, current NIH administrators and scientists asserted that there were no major differences in the functions performed by U.S. and foreign postdoctoral scientists at NIH, except for some minor assignments. One observed that "U.S. fellows do more solo writing, whereas foreign ones tend to need help from senior staff." Work patterns that at first glance may appear to be determined by differences in functions may result, in fact, from alternative approaches and outlooks. One interviewee related that "Americans don't feel rushed because they feel they may have more time—there is no finite time by which they have to leave the United States." Foreign scientists, on the other hand, are aware that their immigration clock is ticking and feel pressured to accomplish as much as they can while at NIH.

Neither were differences in functions seen as significant by former NIH administrators and scientists, aside from those associated with English fluency which makes it easier for American scientists to be assigned leadership roles, including report writing. Also, American M.D.s were viewed as having a broader range of options as to the work they can perform, mostly because of their ability to become involved in clinical issues.

The vast majority of current NIH foreign trainees were emphatic in stating that there were no appreciable differences in the functions performed at NIH by American and foreign scientists. If there is any difference, a Yugoslav entomologist noted, it is that

> Many U.S. employees working at NIH [do so] either in a higher or a lower level than Visiting Associate and Visiting Fellow which are positions often occupied by foreign scientists. And the reason is that Visiting Associates and Visiting Fellows are considered as temporary positions, which many U.S. scientists are not very interested [in]. Furthermore, higher level positions (lab head or administrative staff) or lower level positions (lab technician) are reserved for federal employees that are not open to foreigners; in addition, these are permanent positions. As a result, Americans often hold positions at these two levels, whereas foreigners are mainly in the intermediate level positions.

Other foreign postdocs felt that Americans are prone to get leadership positions and the best work assignments. They attribute this to the fact that Americans are better at interacting and negotiating, as well as in communicating and giving presentations. Foreign scientists viewed Americans as more assertive and aggressive. Ultimately, one person reasoned, NIH promotes Americans in preference to foreigners.

Among those former NIH foreign trainees remaining in the United States, there was consensus regarding the functions of American and foreign postdocs at NIH. All postdocs were viewed as performing essentially similar functions, except that Americans are often given preference for written assignments. Since foreign scientists often have an imperfect knowledge of English, such functions are naturally best assigned to American postdocs. The latter are asked as well to do most of the presentations, whereas foreign postdocs tend to conduct more experiments than Americans. These individuals also noted that if some differences in function are seen, they usually reflect the preferences of laboratory chiefs and personality traits, as well as the background and training of particular postdoctoral scientists.

Working Conditions

Most interviewees did not perceive any differences in working conditions between foreign and U.S. scientists, other than those motivated by the habit of many foreign scientists to work long hours. The tendency to work longer hours was said to be culturally determined in some cases, but also reflected the fact that most foreign postdoctoral trainees come to the Bethesda campus without their families. Since they have no option other than to remain at NIH while on their temporary visas and no family to go to, many foreign postdoctoral trainees engross themselves in their work.

Current and former NIH administrators and scientists emphasized that no differences in work conditions exist at NIH and that this is so by design. One scientist noted that foreign fellows are initially more closely supervised. A foreign-born scientist, now a naturalized American citizen currently working as an NIH contract worker, observed that foreign scientists work harder because:

> Foreign graduate students can obtain a green card only by taking a postdoc or having an employer pay big money to sponsor them. Foreign grad students wishing to stay in the United States are effectively an indentured labor pool, in contrast to grad students with citizenship or permanent visas. At NIH, and certainly at my institute, this does not translate into exploitative working conditions. At other institutions, I believe that it does.

One senior lab chief noted that while there might not be any differences today, NIH did pay lower salaries to foreign scientists after the Second World War. "People from Europe and Japan came from these war-torn regions, and NIH could hire brilliant scientists for less than Americans. Among other advantages gained, NIH survived with all its vigor because of the visiting scientists programs."

No differences in working conditions were reported either by current NIH American trainees. Aside from the observation that foreigners' visa restrictions prevented foreign postdocs from pursuing outside work, no other major differences in working conditions distinguished foreign from American trainees.

The overwhelming majority of the current NIH foreign trainees felt that there are no significant working condition differences at NIH between foreign and American scientists, other than the fact that many foreigners are seen as working longer hours. Fairly typical was the explanation provided by a Canadian physicist when he said "foreigners work longer hours than Americans. Nothing forces us to work longer; it is culturally determined. I usually work 12–14 hours like the French and the Japanese." Another typical response was that of a Chinese scientist when he observed that foreign scientists, such as the Chinese and the Japanese, work longer hours to show their competence and because "they come from cultural traditions of hard work, of being 'industrious.'" Several of the foreign scientists also explained that they had no choice, as Americans do, since given their visa status, they cannot just walk away from NIH and find a job elsewhere in the United States. One interesting difference commented upon by a foreign postdoc is that Fogarty fellows must spend an inordinate amount of time dealing with administrative and immigration-related problems that affect their research performance.

Former NIH foreign trainees who had returned to their countries detected no major differences in working conditions between American and foreign trainees. As one noted, working conditions are generally excellent, although at times the self-imposed work demands are excessive. The availability of resources and the latest technologies increase the willingness to work. Everyone is under constant pressure to perform and produce results, at the same time that they must periodically publish. A former trainee reported that they were expected to work on Saturdays, Sundays, and holidays, and workdays were long. Teamwork was not all it could have been, and instead everyone worked on his or her own. One person vividly described how American and foreigners all work alike: "Like animals," she said.

Several informants observed that scientific techniques and procedures are universal in nature. Despite differences in availability of resources, scientific techniques do not vary from one lab to the next. Some of the differences may be related to cultural characteristics, and how in each culture people approach work. Spanish, Italians, and

French, according to one informant, are very emotional, whereas Asians—Japanese in particular—are very emotionally restrained. Europeans are great at teamwork, and to a lesser extent, so are Americans. Japanese, however, have difficulties working as a team, mostly because they come from a society where hierarchy plays a very important role. However, a number of scientists stressed that these differences, rather than interfering with work at NIH, enrich it. Some felt that working conditions may vary as a function of many factors, including the lab chief, competition within the lab, stage of research project, personalities, and cultural traits of individual investigators.

It was remarked that there are many institutional rules regarding what is and what is not appropriate. Labor laws are rigorously observed and apply to all Americans and foreigners, staff, and trainees alike. Safety procedures must be followed, and everyone must take courses dealing with, for example, safety issues and the handling of laboratory animals. Regulations are rigid and enforced to prevent accidents and other problems that could lead to legal action. Working conditions in specific labs depend on other factors. Some labs are kept less clean and things are handled more carelessly than in others, but all are under constant pressure to adhere to proper procedures. But again, much depends on the lab chief, type of lab, and social environment.

Working conditions are closely correlated with disciplines or specialization. The following characterization is a composite derived from comments made by many of the interviewees. The pace of work is influenced by how long a postdoc has been at a laboratory. When fellows first arrive they feel that they are been evaluated. Thus, during the first year, the work pace is generally more intense and stressful. Working conditions very much depend on whom one works for and other factors related to each specific lab. Someone handling animals, for instance, might be forced to go to the lab on weekends and holidays. Working conditions vary according to the rhythm of work within each lab and demands made by lab chiefs. At times, the number of hours worked is irrelevant: The intensity of work is what counts. When publications are being readied, there are not enough hours in the day. In most labs, work schedules are largely determined by productivity. The dictum of "publish or perish" dominates the lives of postdoctoral trainees at NIH. Failure to publish is a sign of professional failure. Time demands are not set by the laboratory chief but by what is required to meet research objectives.

Compensation

Current NIH administrators and scientists state categorically that the sole bases for determining remuneration at NIH are seniority, rank, or whether a scientist is a postdoctoral trainee or permanent staff member. Compensation differentials vary only as a function of postdoctoral seniority, rank, and tenure status. Higher stipends are also provided to lure physicians to engage in clinical research. Tax-related exemptions enjoyed by nationals of certain countries effectively increase their take-home pay relative to that of other postdocs, including Americans. Some other compensation differences are said to be the result of the aggressiveness of individual scientists or to depend on funding source. According to one American scientist,

> Americans are the more likely to ask for a raise and sometimes they get the raise. Foreigners are not there long enough to ask for a raise. Given enough time, they would be just as pushy as Americans. Sometimes salaries differ because some foreigners are funded by their own country's institutions. Some of the Japanese here at NIH make so little but they are paid by their government not NIH, so there is nothing they can do. One of the Japanese makes a lot of money because he is an associate of a company that sent him over. But the other Japanese man makes very little.

As a general rule, current NIH foreign trainees demonstrated a clear understanding of pay scales at NIH. They were aware of the differences between staff positions and research fellowships, and they grasped the roles played by the Fogarty Center and the IRTA fellowship program. Several also reported than some income differentials are attributed to whether or not foreign fellows pay taxes, and the type of support they have while doing postdoctoral work at NIH (that is, whether they receive a Fogarty stipend or funding from their own governments or industry). For example, a German postdoc described his own situation as follows:

> It is dependent on whether or not the person is paid by Fogarty or by their home country. I was offered funding by both, but decided to choose Fogarty because it paid better than Germany. Also, if you are funded by your country, you are obliged to return. You also earn more if you are a staff worker instead of a Visiting Fellow. Either foreigners or Americans can be [contracted] workers. It does not have to be a permanent position. It is

renewed every year. I don't think this is good because it encourages people to cheat on research results so they will impress the scientific community and get their contract renewed.

Nevertheless, some foreign postdocs voiced complaints about being deprived of long-term benefits that come with permanent staff positions, and still others alleged that some foreign scientists snub NIH because its pay scale is very low. European physicians, in particular, may sense that they are being penalized.

For many, if not most, foreign postdoctoral trainees, whether or not there are compensation differences between themselves and their fellow American counterparts is of no major consequence. They come to NIH to invest in their futures. Launching one's career from NIH is an attractive option since NIH offers young scientists the opportunity to hone their skills, publish in scientific journals, make connections, and wait for the right employment opportunity. At times NIH also acts as a holding pen for young scientists unable to land research positions at home. In the words of a German pharmaceutical chemist, "the money is not the reason why Europeans come to NIH. I know Germans come to NIH because there are much fewer postdocs in Germany. Only the very rich institutions can afford to have postdocs. Institutions such as Max-Planck Institute. So a German comes to the United States if he or she could not get a postdoc or a job in Germany."

Former NIH foreign trainees that have departed the United States believed that there are compensation differences between U.S. and foreign NIH scientists, but they understood these differences to be mostly related to the tax treatment accorded to fellows from different nationalities. For example, some countries have treaties with the United States that permit foreign postdocs to waive taxes, while others do not. Stipends also vary according to years of seniority since fellows are provided with annual increments. Also, it was pointed out that many foreign fellows continue receiving their home country salaries but do not declare them in order to increase their income and avoid paying taxes. Permanent staff receive higher compensation, of course, than postdoctoral trainees, regardless of nationality. For a vast majority of the fellows, however, the level of compensation was not a major concern; they were pleased to be at NIH because of the training and research opportunities it provides.

An interesting issue raised by a few individuals was how much money they had received through their fellowships as compared to what they could have earned in their own countries. One Australian noted that scholarships pay enough to live in the United States, although they tend to be higher in Australia, even if taxes are included. In contrast, an Argentinean remarked that as a NIH fellow she made three times as much as what she currently earns as a full-fledged professional in Buenos Aires.

Former NIH foreign trainees remaining in the United States were of the opinion that stipends at NIH were basically the same for foreign and U.S. scientists. Stipend scales are similar for foreign and American postdoctoral trainees and they vary according to experience and time spent at NIH. Some minor differences in compensation were attributed to whether or not the trainee pays taxes, and if so, to what extent. Payment of taxes varies according to type of visa, with many foreign scientists having a larger paycheck since by treaty they are not under obligation to pay U.S. taxes. Tax exempt status works to the detriment of some postdocs, however. For example, while German nationals are exempt from U.S. taxes, they must pay taxes at a higher rate in their homeland.

Summary

There was general agreement across informant categories that American and foreign biomedical scientists are generally equally qualified, although they may differ in some respects because of training approaches and traditions. Foreign scientists from some countries were said to be more advanced in their training upon arrival at NIH primarily because of a prior more specialized education, in contrast to the broader liberal arts approach followed in the American educational system.

- Foreign biomedical postdoctoral trainees from certain Asian countries and the former Soviet bloc were judged to have stronger backgrounds in mathematics and physics, whereas Europeans have stronger theoretical training. American postdocs, on the other hand, were said to be generally better trained in laboratory techniques and to be more research results oriented.
- There was virtual unanimity across all informant categories that foreign postdocs appear to be more motivated and to work harder than Americans. This is particularly the case among East Asians, most notably, Japanese. This distinction is often attributed to cultural expectations regarding work ethic.
- No significant differences between American and foreign postdocs in disciplines and specialty area were noted, other than a preponderance of

foreign scientists in the relatively new and rapidly growing field of computational biology.

- The functions performed at NIH by American and foreign postdocs were seen as essentially the same. The only difference of note was that because foreign postdocs often lack fluency in English, American trainees more often than not are chosen to make presentations and write technical reports.

- Working conditions were reported as similar, varying only according to specific lab assignments and depending on how individual laboratories are managed.

- Compensation for American and foreign postdocs at NIH was thought to be basically the same. Minor differences may be attributed to whether or not foreign scientists benefit from income tax waivers established by international treaties. Other differences arise when foreign postdocs are paid by their governments or employers, rather than by the U.S. government through one of the foreign postdoctoral programs managed by NIH.

Implications for Employment Prospects and Conditions of American Scientists

Current NIH administrators and scientists addressed this issue with difficulty. Most of them were aware of the complexities of the matter; while some leaned toward concluding that there could be some adverse implications, most felt that the implications were either neutral or beneficial for U.S. scientists over the long term.

The following two statements, both made by lab chiefs, illustrate the complexity of the issue and the logic of the interviewees' perspectives.

[This is] a difficult question to answer because, frankly, job prospects for biological scientists are no longer as promising as they were some years ago. Part of the problem might be an oversupply of scientists, or the fact that most scientifically trained individuals prefer certain types of employment. (e.g., university research labs) over others (e.g., private industry). Some fault may also lie at the foot of universities; they continue to train Ph.D.s and don't tell students the labor market situation is tighter. Funding for science is another factor that contributes to the current situation. The short answer is that foreign scientists may make finding work for U.S. scientists more difficult, but the answer is not clear-cut.

It depends on the educational level at which the hiring is done. At the postdoctoral fellow level, hiring foreign scientists does not influence employment prospects and conditions of U.S. scientists. There are not enough

American scientists available. However, if they [foreign scientists] stay in the U.S., it will have influence, because there will be more competition for scarce jobs. At the permanent residence status, yes. At the senior employment level, there is more competition.

Among those informants who concluded that there were no adverse employment consequences, the reasoning rested on the regulated temporary presence of foreign postdocs at NIH. For instance, one stated, "No effect. The foreign scientists that come to NIH are not permanent. Most return and get positions. Hardly any convert to permanent status." Another emphasized that "NIH encourages foreigners to go back to their home country," while a third said that "virtually all foreign scientists return to their home countries."

Others, however, offered diametrically opposed views. One claimed that "most foreign scientists at NIH as postdoctoral trainees will remain in the United States and compete with U.S. citizen scientists in the same job market."

Some NIH scientists added that there is no impact simply because the foreign scientists fill positions for which no American scientists are available. One lab chief declared, for example, that for now there is not much competition. "Applications for fellowships are running 35 to one foreign versus American." "This shift," he went on, "has taken place since 1975. A vacuum has been created. Americans have been choosing easier disciplines, such as business and law, which lead to more money with less effort."

Yet, others emphasized the benefits that accrue to American biomedical science, and by extension to American scientists, by the presence of foreign scientists, implying that they contribute to job creation for U.S. scientists, although at times they also may increase competition for available work. "Bringing the best people from all over the world to the United States keeps investment capital in the country, increasing the number of industry positions. Bringing more people also makes competition for any given position more rigorous; that is, if your foreign scientists increase the size of the pie but decrease the share reserved for U.S. scientists." A similar view, but with a somewhat different twist, was expressed by a biochemist lab chief: "If a company wants to hire scientists, and if there is no competition from foreign scientists, there is less competition for U.S. scientists. Some Americans have excellent qualifications, but there is a larger pool for selection. In the long run, it is good for this country because it tends to pick up the cream from the world." Another noted, "In theory, it creates more competition. Is this good or bad? It raises the overall level of competence, but it is a problem for Americans because it reduces the availability of academic positions. However, there are other options and English speakers have more advantages." In fact, one lab chief indicated that he was more than likely to give preference to American over foreign job applicants when filling a vacancy. As he noted,

> It is the reverse. If I can find a U.S. citizen I prefer them. The impact is not great because I prefer U.S. scientists because I can find out more about them because I have the connections to find out about them.

Another view was that foreign scientists complement American scientists. "NIH is a mecca for scientists of the world," a NIH scientist commented. "It's not that U.S. scientists are being pushed out. We are all scientists who speak the same language."

The viewpoints of former NIH administrators and scientists were similar. To one former lab chief, the ready availability of foreign scientists "is an easy way of building staff since immediate labor needs are being met." He was nonetheless concerned about the long-term viability of this approach since it precludes developing the proper incentive structure to create opportunities for Americans. He reasoned that this may prove costly in the long term because the United States may eventually discover that it will have to rely more and more on foreign scientists. The position of another former NIH administrator was more positive. Because of the presence of foreign scientists, American educational institutions, she believes, are more likely to produce excellence in certain areas. If American scientists cannot compete, then "tough luck." Despite the fact that NIH still manages to attract some of America's "best biomedical scientists, it has become a far less selective institution than in the past." This was attributed in part to competition from better-paying private industry, a development that helps explain why so many foreign scientists, rather than Americans, are now found at the NIH campus.

Current NIH American trainees felt that their career opportunities at the institutes were extremely limited, but they did not think that the presence of foreign postdocs was a major limiting factor. This point is illustrated by the following three comments:

> Before, there were fiefdoms, and people in power manipulated the process. They would prolong people's hopes, only to drop them later. Now, the process is more open. The new message is 'don't expect a long-term home, only training.'

> There are long-term issues of visa status for scientists who want to stay. They need the support of NIH for visa extensions. NIH is not particularly good at supporting extensions. Now in an era of limited funding, the focus is on training, rather than building the institution. The institution isn't growing, so foreign scientists have to go home, or find another institution to support the visa conversion. New hires at NIH are through attrition.

> A very small number stay as permanent staff. Foreign scientists come for 2–3 years, then with good performance, petition for extension to 5 years. After that it is very difficult to get a permanent job. The recruitment process for permanent positions at NIH is high profile, national, and applicants come from all over. It is a very tight job market. It is rare for foreign scientists to get permanent positions above the postdoc level.

However, looking beyond the situation at NIH, most American trainees felt strongly that once foreign scientists are in the United States, they will begin, sooner or later, to compete for jobs with U.S. scientists. Here are a couple of their remarks:

> I think NIH and the U.S. government are so focused on producing a product that they do not even realize the disservice they are doing to American scientists and the job market. There is a problem when you need a Ph.D. to get a low-level service job. Everyone ends up overqualified.

> The same thing that happened to math, physics, and astronomy is happening to biology. My husband had a ten-year postdoc. It was the influx of foreigners (Russians) at the end of the Cold War that caused the degree inflation in physics and astronomy, and it will be the influx of foreigners that will cause it in biology. The Russians at NCI are physicists. This inflation is a waste of societal resources. And even though things are good now for NCI this is just a trend, a flavor of the month. The flavor of the month usually lasts about 5 years. Everyone hears computational biology has tons of job openings and everyone goes into computational biology and floods the job market. Leaving computational biology right where the rest of biology is right now—in a depressed job market.

Current NIH American trainees viewed the issue of potential competition from foreign scientists with ambivalence. Many were torn between positive feelings toward fellow foreign colleagues on a personal level and negative considerations about the presence of foreigners on an occupational level. The conclusion for some was that "if the current trend is allowed to continue, all the leading positions in science will be held by foreigners. I think this is because NIH is cherry picking from the world and the talent level is so high." This conclusion arose in part from the realization that many of the foreign scientists are not going home. As one interviewee noted,

> The problem becomes that we have equally trained foreign and American people for the same jobs. This is the dilemma of being an open democracy. I don't think we should legislate it, but I think we should implement a fruitful dialogue and then make a decision. The NIH has global health concerns and so needs to attract the best scientists and this can only be done without boundaries. NIH takes a balanced position and they should try not to veer to either side and should fight to retain diversity and social cohesion.

Other individuals commented that postdocs currently face a difficult time with limited growth in academic jobs and a growing surplus of Ph.D.s. In the view of one, American science has done a good job in developing and applying technology, to the point that not all technology jobs could be filled. However, he went on,

> We are top-heavy with Ph.D.s and how do we match academic degrees given to jobs available that require that level of education? I think M.D.s are a little different. They are not as willing to make the sacrifice and to go for the Ph.D. and enter a bad job market. There is no doubt that there is a limited set of resources and by accepting foreign postdocs the competition for these resources goes up. But I do not think that limiting or preventing foreign scientists from coming to America is the answer.

This same ambivalence was revealed by another American postdoc who concluded that the oversupply of biomedical scientists has both endogenous and exogenous origins. In his words, "NIH needs foreign scientists in terms of quantity, quality, and motivation. It is a trade-off, and it doubtless costs some American jobs. But free competition is the American way. As they say, 'Be a leader or get out of the way.'"

Such personal ambivalence was poignantly expressed by a man in his late thirties who was completing his third and final NIH fellow-ship:

> An unlimited talent pool of scientists makes it difficult for U.S. scientists because it creates an unstable job market. In between an increased labor pool and tenure, I'm out [of academia]. However, overall, I think it is for the best: for the United States, for the advance and globalization of scientific knowledge, and in about 20 years from now when I'm older, probably best for my health, too.

In the main, former NIH American trainees did not perceive foreign scientists as a factor that might limit their own career opportunities. As one observed, "having foreign trainees at NIH does not restrict the opportunities of American trainees for getting permanent positions at NIH, which is very hard to do, regardless." Others minimized the labor market impact of foreign scientists by drawing attention to the obstacles they must overcome if they wish to remain in the United States. Typical of this sentiment was the following observation:

> By virtue of having more well-trained scientists in the country, there is of course going to be more competition. However, because foreigners have to jump through hoops to attain legal residence, there is more work involved in hiring them, and this favors Americans.

Still another perspective emphasized the fact that American and foreign scientists fill different labor market niches. A comment along this line ran as follows:

> I don't think they hold any implications because I think Americans are filling the R&D company and industry positions because they are interested in making money. Plus, in industry you have to be able to think on your feet. Americans are good at this because our culture encourages this behavior.

Others, however, saw a mixed picture. The next two statements show that bringing foreign scientists to this country can be interpreted as a mixed blessing:

> Most of them go back home, but the Indians stay and the Chinese stay. The opportunities are limited for them back home. In the United States, we have the rise and expansion of biotechnology, and certain special areas

like bioinformatics are burgeoning. It is logical that they would want to stay here . . . This creates a squeeze in academia, and therefore many are leaving academia and going to work for the new biotech companies.

For Americans, this has a lot of advantages. It opens up communication with the rest of the world. It benefits us economically and scientifically. The current stress on multiculturalism promotes positive attitudes toward foreigners. However, this situation, like having clinical residencies filled with high numbers of foreigners, has to be looked at carefully: The competition [represented by the foreign trainees] is good for the country, but it makes life personally difficult for the Americans who have to compete.

Among the current NIH foreign trainees, some claimed not to have a ready answer regarding the labor market impact of foreign scientists, whereas the rest were equally divided between those who believed the consequences to be negative or positive. Those who perceived adverse effects for American scientists evinced straightforward reasoning. They assumed an opportunity pie of a constant size in which the entry of additional workers increases competition for available positions. The negative effects were seen as manageable, however. Of foreign scientists coming to NIH, only a small portion were believed to remain in the United States. Further, as some American postdocs remarked, even if foreign scientists stay in this country, they are at a relative disadvantage vis-à-vis American scientists because the latter are more skilled at communicating and have better access to U.S. professional networks. In addition, Americans do not have to face the visa hurdles that foreign scientists must confront. In some fields, such as general biology, competition is intense, whereas in some narrow specialties like cellular biology, where few new positions are available, competitive pressures are accentuated. Overall, the gist was that an abundant supply of foreign competitors is to the detriment of American scientists since it places them at a disadvantage when bargaining with potential employers and because labor market competition for individual scientists will increase. However, the country as a whole and the biomedical science profession in particular should benefit as the United States increases its edge in international competitiveness.

For those who judged that there are no adverse consequences, several reasons were given. One is that the United States would not invite foreign scientists to NIH unless they were needed. That is, there is a shortage of U.S. scientists, and foreign scientists fill the void.

"It is a matter of supply and demand," a Russian biochemist concluded. A Ukrainian molecular biologist echoed this sentiment by noting that "the American job market is good so I don't think foreigners have a lot of influence on it." At NIH, you can categorically say there is no competition, said an Indian computational biologist, since U.S. and foreign scientists fill different labor market niches, with foreign scientists generally being found at the bottom of a pyramidal hierarchy. For some, the issue was irrelevant. Visiting Fellows occupy training slots, not formal staff positions. And, it was pointed out, INS tightly regulates the number of foreign biomedical scientists that are allowed to remain in the United States.

Among the former NIH foreign trainees who had returned to their countries, most believed that the presence of foreign biomedical trainees at NIH does not threaten employment prospects and conditions for U.S. scientists. First, most of the foreign trainees at NIH choose to return home. Second, "NIH is not attractive for Americans." This latter theme was emphasized by many of the former trainees interviewed abroad. As a thirty-seven-year-old Argentinean biologist observed, the "tendency among U.S. scientists is to go to private industry given that they are not interested in basic research. In basic research the pay is low and American culture emphasizes earning high salaries." Those espousing this view also occasionally observed that immigration regulations closely control the entry of foreign scientists and that the tenure track process ensures that only the very best foreign trainees remain at NIH. In brief, "it is the United States that does the selection." Further, it was asserted, the presence of foreign scientists has no bearing on the conditions of American scientists since the Fogarty system provides for a quota of foreign scientists, while NIH allocates a fixed set of postdoctoral training appointments for U.S. scientists. In addition, even though there are many biomedical scientists in the United States, there are not enough of them willing to fill vacancies at NIH laboratories.

Perhaps a more dominant view among these overseas scientists was that the employment prospects of American scientists improve thanks to the presence of foreign biomedical scientists at NIH. According to this line of reasoning, "NIH generates a very dynamic scientific culture highly beneficial to American society. The productivity of foreign fellows is high because they do not go to NIH to waste time, they are anxious to learn, to create knowledge, and to publish." Furthermore,

NIH and the American biomedical scientific establishment "need people, many people, and they don't care if one is American or foreigner." The ebb and flow of young scientists at NIH is so dynamic, commented one person, that "the bosses sometimes don't even recognize their own fellows."

While some mentioned that the presence of foreign scientists at NIH and their eventual permanent settlement in the United States could in fact result in more labor market competition for native scientists, they reasoned that over the long haul this is a self-correcting process. The scientific contributions made by foreign scientists translate into a wave of rising employment. In any case, the United States needs more "hands" than are available domestically.

A good many of the former NIH foreign trainees staying in the United States disagreed with the notion that the presence of foreign postdoctoral trainees has an adverse impact on the employment prospects and working conditions of U.S. scientists. They felt that NIH does not expect foreign scientist on J–1 or F–1 visas to remain in the United States and, furthermore, they believed that in order to obtain a NIH tenure track appointment, a permanent residence visa is required. "Since Visiting Fellow and Visiting Associate positions are exclusively for foreign scientists," one person of Chinese origin said, "the imagined"'competition' between foreign and U.S. scientists does not exist." From this perspective, the effect is minimal since the INS presumably keeps a tight leash on foreign scientists.

Others recognized, however, that a postdoctoral appointment often opens the gate for permanent U.S. residence, as in their own cases. This was the situation with one European scientist who had lived and worked in the United States for seven years under several types of visas and who was seeking a green card at the time he was interviewed. Although he concluded that the limited number of NIH postdocs remaining in the United States can hardly be expected to have a major detrimental impact on U.S. scientists, he felt that "it cannot be disputed that anyone coming in takes resources and takes away from people already there."

Others saw a direct relationship between the presence of foreign biomedical scientists at NIH and other research facilities. Based on her experience with foreign postdoctoral trainees, a Swedish-born scientist concluded that most want to remain in the United States. In some specialty fields, such as general and cellular biology, she thought that

U.S. scientists should be upset because the demand for jobs far exceeds the supply. This view is in sharp contrast with that expressed by an Indian scientist who claimed that there are plenty of jobs for all qualified biomedical scientists. From his perspective, the American job market is competitive, and foreigners and Americans are in the same boat. "Jobs should be based on merit, and employers should hire the best person for the job, the most productive person."

Some interviewees pointed out that the impact of the employment of foreign scientists on U.S. scientists should not be viewed in isolation. A sensible judgment at any given time must be sensitive to the prevailing economic situation, in particular the unemployment rate. They noted that with demand for biomedical scientists extremely high in the late 1990s, there seemed to be no negative impact on the job prospects of Americans.

Summary

Persons in all interview categories regarded with ambivalence the impact that the presence of foreign scientists at NIH and in the United States more generally has on the employment prospects and conditions of American scientists.

- With regard to NIH specifically, the preponderant view was of no impact since the temporary admission of postdoctoral fellows and other foreign scientists is tightly regulated by several U.S. government agencies (NIH, INS). Further, foreign scientists qualified to apply for the few tenure-track career appointment positions must openly compete through a highly structured and transparent process.

Beyond the confines of NIH, labor market impact assessments were more contorted. They tacitly assumed that foreign scientists use temporary training visas (at NIH and other institutions) or other types of visas (at other institutions, such as F–1s at universities) as a bridge to permanent visas. Labor market impact assessments were also highly dependent on the varying time perspectives of different individuals. In general, however, most minimized the adverse labor market impacts of foreign scientists. Their views may be summarized as follows:

- While many believed that foreign scientists increase labor market competition over the short-term, they were confident that more scientific jobs are generated over the long-term as a result of foreigners' contributions to U.S. scientific prowess and to American international competitiveness in biomedical research and biotechnology.

- A corollary point was that although competition from foreign scientists might be detrimental for individual American scientists, their presence benefits the broader American scientific enterprise and thus the country at large.
- Some were concerned that because of the presence of foreign scientists in the U.S. labor market, a process of credential creep in biomedical research is underway.
- Foreigners occupy different labor market niches than do Americans and are unlikely to displace them given the latter's greater English language and communication skills, as well as labor market knowledge and contacts.

However, some persons were convinced that

- The influx of foreign scientists was already having a damaging impact on the employment prospects of American scientists.

Implications for American Training Institutions

The dominant view expressed by current NIH administrators and scientists regarding the implications arising from the presence of foreign biomedical trainees at NIH for U.S. training institutions and national expertise in science was generally positive, particularly if the scientists were to remain in the United States. Adverse effects could result, however, if foreign scientists, especially those from advanced industrial countries, returned to their home countries. As one NIH scientist observed:

> To the degree that they go home, it increases competition; but their being here helps us advance. For example, Japanese biomedicine has improved, but there is a trade off, in that the competition it creates is healthy for U.S. research. Also, continuing contact and collaboration helps in the long run. This is how science is done, and it allows breakthroughs. For example, NIH mentors and former fellows often collaborate in research, which sometimes leads to the development of new drugs.

From some perspectives, the presence of foreign scientists is not necessarily beneficial. Several noted that it is a myth that NIH and other U.S. training institutions host only "the best and brightest." As one stated, "Many of the scientists who come to the United States are run-of-the-mill and do not make contributions significantly greater than what would be expected from the average U.S. scientist." Another reinforced this perspective by noting the very large number of applications that NIH receives from scientists in mainland China who are "doing totally unrelated work [and are] just looking for a job to get . . . into the United States."

The possibility of a glut of biomedical scientists in the U.S. labor market was also raised. Several felt that the benefits to American educational institutions are limited or ephemeral at best, and often accrue to the benefit of only established scientists. In the words of one interviewee,

> Foreign nationals with work permission lower the cost of labor for the glutted academic job market, without increasing overall university resources slated for paying academics. I think that academia is pretty grim right now, for reasons only weakly related to the influx of foreign scientists. The only people that benefit from the current situation are deans and boards of trustees.

According to this viewpoint, foreign scientists are taking positions from U.S. scientists at these institutions, but they are no better qualified than available American scientists.

NIH's practice of offering postdoctoral training fellowships to foreign scientist mirrors the trend of enrolling an increasing number of foreign students at U.S. universities. Many of these come to train at NIH after graduating and eventually settle in this country. Of the foreign scientists coming to NIH directly from their home academic institutions, one individual observed, very few really have a chance to stay there because of the recent establishment of very competitive hiring procedures. This may create a problem for the less assertive of the foreign scientists, but this situation is not different from similar problems faced by U.S. scientists.

While many felt that there might be some benefits to hiring foreign scientists, they were conservative in assessing what these might entail. Several mentioned low costs, while others referred to the positive effects that expanding the pool of available scientists has, particularly when there is a shortage of American scientists. One commented, for instance, that "there are more foreign applicants to work at my lab than domestic scientists. It is a supply and demand market." Another indicated that there are "not enough American graduating students in the sciences. NIH and scientific institutions are dying to get more scientists, but do not have enough." By the same token, some scientists felt that "if domestic scientists apply and have the same credentials, domestic scientists would be given preference."

Opinions were divided among former NIH administrators and scientists regarding the impact that foreign postdoctoral trainees and scientists have on U.S. training institutions. On one hand, there are those who see a negative, or, at best, neutral impact. Many thought that the large influx of foreign scientists would have a negative impact on Americans by dissuading many future students from going to graduate school to pursue advanced biomedical degrees. The end result will be a contraction in the number of Americans enrolling for Ph.D.s in these fields at U.S. universities, as has occurred in engineering and the physical sciences. In due course, this could only reduce American scientific output. It is a vicious circle that feeds itself. As one former NIH administrator observed, the proportion of highly trained foreigners who stay here is usually higher among those who come from less developed countries, whether from the Caribbean, Brazil, China, India, or Africa, who are unable to use their new skills in their home countries, which simply do not have appropriate technical facilities. Instead, these foreigners stay and compete for jobs here. Hence, budding American scientists will have even less incentive to engage in rigorous biomedical training.

Current and former NIH American trainees were very favorable in their opinions about the implications of having foreign scientists brought to the United States. They saw them as contributing positively to American training institutions, national expertise, and international competitiveness in biomedical science.

The bulk of current NIH foreign trainees had no hesitation when addressing this issue. They felt that U.S. training institutions and national expertise in biomedical science benefit significantly from the presence of foreign scientists in American research laboratories. National capabilities are sharpened by exposure to and competition with foreign scientists regardless of the size and expertise of the existing domestic scientific pool. In the words of a German trainee, foreign scientists represent a great chance for the United States since "it is getting so many talented foreign scientists to increase the level of science being done in the United States." Their presence helps establish an ever-higher standard. A Korean molecular biologist added that American science benefits, "since scientists, no matter were they are from, increase their skills through interchanges with other scientists."

The vast majority of former foreign trainees who returned home concluded that American training institutions benefit greatly from the presence of foreign scientists at NIH and in the United States more generally. The reasons given for these conclusions were varied and ranged from arguments that suggest that many advantages accrue from the conduct of multicultural research, to the prevalent view that NIH, as well as other U.S. training institutions, can evaluate and select the most brilliant foreign scientists while they are in training at NIH.

As related by an Argentinean biologist, "the presence of foreign scientists increases the army of researchers needed by U.S. science. Many foreign scientists see in academia the opportunity of staying. Foreign scientists who state at the outset that they want to return to the home countries are looked at with surprise. Most who aspire to stay are from countries with only limited opportunities. Italians, French, and Spaniards usually complain, but generally return to their home countries." This individual also felt that it is relatively easy for foreign postdocs to obtain positions in second-rate American universities, as compared to well-paying academic positions in their native countries. A similar view was offered by another former NIH fellow who thought U.S. investigators are only interested in working at prestige universities and not in those of lesser rank. Since U.S. universities are so varied in terms of reputation, he reasoned, the least prestigious are shunned by American scientists, while foreigners are content with working in those that are ranked lowest. Therefore, there is no competition. Another widely held view was that the hiring of foreign scientists at these educational institutions—with different skills due to differences in training—creates an atmosphere in which American scientists and students learn new ways of doing things. All of this results in better biomedical research and leads to even more linkages with foreign scientists.

The majority of former NIH foreign trainees remaining in the United States also believed that the presence of foreign scientists at NIH and other American research institutions benefits the United States. Since the foreign scientists that come to the United States are selected for their skills, the level of scientific discourse is raised and the bar for scientific discoveries lowered. The United States also benefits since most of these scientists were educated at the expense of other countries and because they bring to American laboratories different approaches to the pursuit of science. Furthermore, since foreign scientists are accustomed to working in research environments with far fewer material and technical resources, they take maximum advantage of U.S. research facilities.

Summary

Many interviewees were of the opinion that American training institutions ought to benefit from the presence of foreign scientists in the United States. The main argument for this view is in fact one of the principal justifications for the establishment of international programs at NIH.

- Training institutions, including NIH, should become more productive through the interaction of American and foreign scientist. The latter bring new ideas and skills to doing things.
- Training institutions, including NIH, are placed in the enviable position of being able to evaluate and choose research staff from a world pool of scientific talent.

The implications are not quite as positive in the view of many if consideration is given to the impact an expanding supply of foreign biomedical scientists is likely to have on the educational plans of American students.

- Many believed that the increasing number of foreign biomedical scientists in the United States—as students, academics, and employees of biotechnology firms—will have detrimental consequences for American training institutions. Due to increased labor market competition, fewer and fewer Americans are likely to follow biomedical research careers, thus forcing the United States into a vicious cycle of dependence on foreign scientists to maintain a technological lead in biomedical research and biotechnology.

Implications for American International Competitiveness in Biomedical Research and Biotechnology

Current NIH administrators and scientists expressed pride in the biomedical advances achieved at NIH, and felt, without exception, that basic biomedical research benefits from the international scientific exchanges sponsored by NIH. Some of them were more hesitant about venturing opinions about the impact of the presence of foreign scientists in the U.S. biotechnology industry, primarily because their work was too far removed from that arena. The dominant thought, nonetheless, was that the U.S. biotechnology industry reaps major benefits. As one observed, "having foreign scientists from all over the globe diversifies the types of research projects conducted at NIH." The effect is beneficial, noted a European-born administrator and scientist, "because it provides a good blend of the American enterprising spirit with the hard work ethics of the immigrant population." While the benefits for the industry are apparent, labor market "competition is the price you pay. But, in principle, it is good: Competition brings out the best, in the best interest of all."

Several factors were assumed to influence whether or not foreign scientists contribute to or detract from U.S. international competitiveness in biotechnology. Where they come from and whence they return were seen as most important. For example, "People from Japan have no trouble returning to work in Japan. It is different with scientists from India. They cannot return because of limitations in hiring. They are more likely to remain. It is rare that a Japanese scientist remains in the U.S." This can also be interpreted to imply that the knowledge acquired by Japanese scientists can lead to more competition for American industry, rather than serve to enhance American competitiveness in the international market place.

Most NIH scientists felt that the presence of foreign biomedical postdoc scientists is beneficial for U.S. scientific research and development firms. One naturalized scientist of Indian background summarized the view of many when he stated, "The implications are excellent! Where is the problem here? Fermi and Einstein weren't native-born Americans, either." Some noted that NIH "provides a rich source for recruitment" for some of the best scientists that can be found anywhere in the world. Others commented that "development firms have more to choose from, and often at lower costs, at least over the short term." Several interviewees asserted that the presence of foreign scientists at NIH is beneficial since they help reduce shortages of U.S. scientists. As one pointed out, "There are not enough American scientists with a postdoctorate. There are not enough national scientists to fill available positions. Scientific institutions cannot function without supply from other countries." It was stressed that this also applies to research firms and universities that actively recruit foreign NIH postdocs.

The benefits for U.S. scientific research largely accrue from the decision of many of the foreign postdocs to remain permanently in the United States. Perceptions of the relative number of foreign biomedical scientists that manage to find sponsors to locate employment and settle in the United States varied considerably. "In my experience, 90 percent return home," said a scientist who felt that the foreign scientist impact was small, whereas another with no clear-cut view on the matter assumed than about half remained. A scientist who believed that the presence of foreign scientists has negative consequences felt that "more scientists are staying in the U.S. They are staying and we are keeping undesirable scientists in this country. Some of the scientists are not necessarily the best trained or have the best scientific motivation. Personal ambition may over-rule scientific ambition."

Most former NIH administrators and scientists saw only the benefits the United States derives from the presence of foreign scientists at NIH and eventually in the American labor force. They pointed out that, as a society, America receives a major infusion of knowledge from abroad that in no way interferes with opportunities for American scientists. They stressed that the research establishment, including the biotechnology industry, gains most. Potential employers get a chance to observe foreign scientists at work in a U.S.-accredited program, are not forced to go abroad to look for them without knowing how well they might adapt to working in this country, and can employ the very best of the lot. Everyone gains: the foreign scientists that get to stay in the United States, the employers, and American society at large. Foreign scientists contribute to the national stock of knowledge and help give America an international competitive edge.

Aside from their own employment concerns, most current NIH American trainees were very favorable in their opinions about the implications of having foreign scientists in the United States. They saw them as contributing positively to American national expertise and international competitiveness in biomedical science. One stated that "it insures the pre-eminence of U.S. institutions. It is positive for national expertise, too." Another pointed out that "the United States gains since our domestic science base is broadened. We learn as much from foreign scientists as they learn from us." And a third referred to America's positive tradition of immigration: "It benefits. Einstein was a foreign scientist. In the long term, it helps America."

Nonetheless, it was noted that this approach to national scientific advancement cannot occur without cost for some Americans. One American postdoc was especially troubled by this trend:

> The future is that people in the highest levels of science will be foreigners. There is an essay on the Internet written by foreign economists concluding that the end result of this trend will be that Americans won't control science in America. This is complete internationalism and will lead to complete disintegration of the U.S. labor force. This is all part of the downward spiral of American education. I believe research has degraded the quality of education. Teaching is an afterthought. In fact, being a good teacher hurts you because you are throwing time away from your research.

Another gave a more positive assessment:

> From the point of view of management, it has the best people coming in— "unfettered labor" is a positive. From the viewpoint of labor, however, the opposite holds true. The United States has the lead in biomedical research, and an open door helps maintain this lead. It is best overall from both a U.S. and a global perspective to have a concentration [of talented scientists] in one country.

Former NIH American trainees were generally favorable in their estimates of the impact of foreign scientists on U. S. training institutions and on American excellence and international competitiveness in biomedicine and biotechnology. One observed that "Most foreign scientists come here for the training because there are not enough institutions in their home country. I think the foreign scientists are helping us because they produce a great amount of quality work at NIH." Another typical comment was that "it makes the United States more competitive because we are recruiting the best of the best and they sometimes end up staying in the U.S. and getting either an academic position or a position in industry."

In regard to potential competition from abroad, the general sense of these scientists was that "the United States is so far ahead of the rest of the world in biomedical science that competition doesn't matter. The idea of technology leakage to other countries has been grossly overestimated."

Current NIH foreign trainees overwhelmingly believed that their presence in the United States and at NIH brings multiple benefits to U.S. scientific research and biotech firms. First, firms have access to a broader pool of scientific talent from which to choose biomedical researchers. Biomedical researchers with NIH experience are very attractive to business firms. A second benefit to firms is that if they hire foreign fellows from NIH, they usually are willing to work harder and for less, and they bring different experiences and ways of doing things to the table.

These positive assessments were somewhat tempered by the observations of others. A Chinese-Canadian scientist enunciated a critical view. "As a country," he said, "the United States will benefit from the hiring and employment of foreign scientists; but, as individuals, American scientists will face more competitors from all over the world, and this will make the job market more competitive." The benefits also seemed more questionable to a Korean biochemist who observed that not every foreign scientist who does postdoctoral work at NIH wishes to remain in the United States. He indicated that the return home of these scientists may imply costs related to the ability of the United States to maintain its international technological lead in biotechnology since those most likely to return home are from competitor countries. As he remarked, "most people from countries in which the research environment is comparable to the United States want to return. It is mostly in countries like China, where the economic situation is very poor, that they are looking to come to America [and stay] because they hear about the kinds of science they are doing here and they know they cannot do that kind of science in their own country." Others referred to the differential propensity of postdocs to remain in the United States or return to the home countries. The differential was usually found at the cleavage separating developed from developing home country.

Current NIH foreign trainees, while not unanimous in their assessments, were overwhelmingly in agreement with the premise that American international competitiveness in biotechnology is enhanced by the presence of foreign biomedical scientists at NIH and other U.S. research facilities. A Canadian endocrinologist provided an emphatic endorsement of this notion when he observed that "there is an immediate payoff by making the United States more capable."

Some foreign postdocs were skeptical. They observed that as long as biomedical research continues to be done as in the past and research results are published in the international scientific literature, it does not much matter where the research is done. As a consequence, therefore, the presence of foreign scientists at NIH does not directly affect U.S. international competitiveness. On the other hand, as one Russian scientist observed, the presence of a large research community at NIH offers considerable advantages to prospective U.S. employers as a fruitful recruitment ground. A French virologist, perhaps reflecting on the experience of other technological sectors where the United States once had the scientific lead but failed to capitalize on it, raised a cautionary flag. It all depends, according to him, on the time perspective, and the extent to which returning scientists take back with them the technological know-how acquired while undergoing training in the United States:

> In the short range, it is positive, and acts like an engine. The long range is more problematic: It depends on the conversion of discoveries into products in the United States. The more this occurs over time, the relatively better is the United States position. But if conversion does not take place in the United States and occurs in other countries, then the United States position is hurt.

Among former NIH foreign postdocs who had returned home, most believed that U.S. biotechnology firms, particularly the small start-up companies, derive significant benefits from the presence of foreign postdoctoral trainees at NIH. They contribute to the basic science advances that stand behind most biotechnology applications. Also, as one person observed, "there is a very strong correlation between the employment of foreign scientists and scientific research and the development of biotechnology firms." NIH acts as a rich source for biotechnology firms that often "work closely with NIH, supply NIH labs, and are always alert looking for the best prospects." One scientist stated, "NIH provides an entry door to an eventual labor market in the commercial biotechnology sector," and another remarked that "the institution is a great factory of scientists." They pointed out that if a promising prospect is identified, U.S. firms are likely to assist the foreign scientist in obtaining a temporary work permit or the coveted green card. Foreign scientists may also be tapped to generate business for the firm abroad, perhaps as a company representative in their home countries where they may possess potentially valuable connections. An important benefit is that these foreign scientists have already been fully trained, and therefore the firms do not have to invest any of their resources in developing these very skilled workers.

The fact that a biomedical scientific and biotechnology commercial corridor has sprung around and near the NIH Bethesda campus was highlighted by several interviewees. Most of the firms in this cluster are small, start-up firms often established by scientists formerly associated with NIH. "This is one of the reasons why so many biotechnology firms are located in the Washington area around the NIH," commented one foreign scientist.

Large R&D firms work with small firms, which often fail to develop and test new products or to assess their commercial viability. Since small firms by and large do not have basic science capabilities, and NIH's mandate is to train people in basic sciences, this places the NIH fellows, most of which are foreigners, in a privileged position. "Biotechnology firms must go to NIH because they do not produce knowledge but they need knowledge to be profitable," said one foreign scientist, while another observed that "NIH hosts an annual fair in which scientists present their research, which is a veritable gold mine for biotechnology firms."

A number of former NIH foreign trainees who had returned home also drew attention to the fact that diversity in research is good and generates competition, not among firms per se, but along lines of investigation that later on firms attempt to exploit by attracting scientists. Foreign scientists, one observed, "are a cheap labor force, are not demanding, and are highly adaptable. Foreign scientists are very committed to their work, work hard and are self demanding, all of which benefits American science." A major drawback of the process from the perspective of some foreign scientists is that "the most talented foreign scientists are hired by the private sector, taking away from the countries of origin a very valuable human resource," to the benefit of the United States.

Interesting changes were noted by several of the older interviewees who had been foreign trainees at NIH several decades ago. A fifty-seven-year-old physician from Argentina noted that twenty years ago, "the biotechnology industry was not as developed as it is now . . . there were not the commercial opportunities that there are currently. The professional pathway was academia." This remark reflects the revolutionary changes experienced by the biomedical sciences since the 1970s and the emergence of the biotechnology industry as one of the most potentially important business enterprises of the twenty-first century.

Without access to so many foreign scientists and the cultural diversity they represent, most returned scientists felt, the United States could not hold the international lead it has in biotechnology. The presence of foreign scientists is advantageous for the United States as well as for foreign investigators, they asserted. The United States gains a competitive advantage by having on a permanent basis a large pool of foreign scientists working under ideal conditions in relation to the rest of the world. This translates into an extraordinary competitive gain, or, in the words of one foreign scientist, "for the United States to hire foreigners constitutes more than a competitive advantage; it is an absolute advantage." Foreign scientists have contributed to the preeminence of the American biotechnology industry in many different ways, stated one previous NIH postdoc interviewed in South America, be it through the work they have done in laboratories or through their entrepreneurial spirit. He buttressed his claim by showing the interviewer a facsimile he had just received from a biotech firm in the United States: "See, the name in the signature is obviously Chinese; underneath it you can clearly note: It says, President."

Foreign scientists, particularly from developing countries, often remarked that working at NIH represented an opportunity to be associated with a center of excellence and the possibility of making higher salaries than in their home countries. This symbiotic relationship is based in part on NIH's scientific breadth. "Each disease has a niche at NIH," observed one informant, who wondered aloud where else in the world could there be such a vast and diverse biomedical center and so many opportunities for applied science. This breadth is fed, noted another, by drawing scientists from all over the world. "Fogarty has offices in practically every country, and in each a local committee that evaluates candidates. It seems like a very intelligent selection approach."

Several interviewees commented that U.S. preeminence in biotechnology is beginning to be challenged abroad, particularly by European competitors, a factor that may be pushing American companies to be even more innovative. Increased competitive pressures may be a factor behind the hiring of so many foreign scientists. In the short term this may be beneficial as long as they stay with U.S. companies; but if they return to their home countries, they may begin to work for competing firms. However, as far as one thirty-two-year-old Australian pharmacologist knew "most biotechnology firms the world over are in one way or another linked to American firms, which means American competitiveness is on the rise." A German scientist added that although over the long haul some non-American firms may benefit, ultimately the United States should emerge as the big winner as the country's productivity is enhanced.

Most of the former NIH foreign trainees who are now located in the United States subscribed to the view that the presence of foreign biomedical scientists in the United States strengthens this country's scientific research capability and its biotechnology firms. One such individual, interviewed during a poster session held during a major molecular biology congress in San Francisco, indicated that most poster presenters were foreign scientists showing those interested what kind of research they were doing and how. Many emphasized that foreign scientists employed in the United States made significant contributions to knowledge and contributed to the development of new commercial products and applications.

Yet, some were more restrained. One thought that the potential contributions of foreign scientists may not be as significant in the future as they may have been in the past since the pace of exponential growth in biomedical knowledge seen during the 1970s has slowed. Another view was that biomedical research done at NIH is of only limited consequence for biotechnology firms given that it is too much oriented toward pure, basic research rather than practical, commercial applications. However, most felt that the international competitiveness of the United States in biomedicine and biotechnology stands to gain much from the presence of foreign biomedical scientists in its laboratories. As one put it, "spend the money, get the knowledge." Another foreign-born scientist alluded to the fact that the U.S. biotechnology industry gains from the contributions made by the cheap labor provided by the foreign postdoctoral trainees who contribute "brain labor." This foreign brain labor is one of the reasons why America is the best in the field of biomedicine, and "foreigners have done this mostly by creating competition." In the view of a Taiwan-born former NIH postdoc who is now a professor at a leading California university, principal investigators at NIH and elsewhere seek foreign scientists "because America is such a wealthy society that its people have lost competitiveness and rest on their laurels and know foreigners will work hard."

Summary

Across the interview categories, there was consensus that basic biomedical scientific research in the United States gains considerably from international exchanges. Thus,

- The presence of foreign scientists at NIH and in other U.S. research laboratories contributes to continued American pre-eminence in biomedicine.

The U.S. biotechnology industry, according to the vast majority of those interviewed, is also a major winner as long as the foreign scientists remain here.

- NIH's foreign training program is generally viewed as contributing to furthering American dominance in biomedical research and biotechnology. NIH serves as an ideal recruiting ground for international scientific talent by giving potential U.S. employers the opportunity to evaluate and select from a large pool of candidates drawn from all world regions that contains the best-qualified and most promising young scientists.
- Foreign biomedical scientists expand the pool of highly skilled scientific talent and help reduce shortages in emerging and specialized fields.
- Foreign scientists not only contribute to biomedical research, they also energize the American economy through their entrepreneurial spirit.

A few expressed concern about scientists from countries with advanced biotechnology industries (e.g., chemistry, pharmaceutical, agronomy) taking home knowledge acquired in the United States. This knowledge might be used to challenge the U.S. biotechnology industry in the international marketplace or could be detrimental if American firms fail to take commercial advantage of basic scientific discoveries made in U.S. laboratories. The great majority, however, thought the likelihood of this occurring to be small.

- American international competitiveness might suffer when and if foreign scientists, including trainees, return to their home countries and apply what they have learned in the United States. But the likelihood is modest.

Implications for American Immigration and Labor Policies

Some current NIH administrators and scientists provided even-handed judgments regarding the implications for U.S. immigration and labor policies of the presence of foreign biomedical scientists at NIH and within the larger American scientific establishment. As one commented, "the answer to this question depends on the balance that is struck between the demand and supply of scientists, funding possibilities, employment options, etc." Another noted,

> It's hard to say. U.S. immigration policy is set by different competing factors big business on one side, which is open to immigration; trade unions, and local politics on the other side trying to restrict it. This sets up a creative tension that works as a compromise. At any rate, immigration is hardly automatic or easy. Are countries that restrict immigration like European countries and Japan better off? They have a much smaller number and percentage of new [business] starts and products and prizes than the United States.

The opinions of many were reflected in the comment of one senior scientist regarding the scientific and economic impact of foreign scientists in the United States labor market: "The U.S. government should make it easier for the highly skilled to come to the U.S. because it is to the advantage of the U.S. to have them here." Some believed that because the scientists involved are so specialized and their numbers are so small, the current state of affairs is appropriate and that no changes in immigration policy are needed. One scientist drew a parallel in observing that many foreign medical doctors are willing to settle in rural areas of the United States where American physicians are unwilling to go.

A few expressed serious concern about the prevailing immigration pattern of foreigners at NIH. One felt the implications to be highly significant because many foreign scientists use NIH as a stepping stone to employment in the U.S. labor market. In his view, the United States "can't get people [scientists] to return to their home countries—consulates are blocking visas with this in mind." However, others thought the rules had become trivial. One remarked, "People have learned to work around it [immigration policy]. Foreigners are supposed to return to their own countries for two years, but that doesn't really make much sense. It's a sham."

Most, however, saw no immigration implications as far as NIH is concerned since "NIH does not often (as do universities) obtain H–1B visas or permanent residences for its employees. Only when they want to hire someone permanently. This is rare and has insignificant effects. For example, of the fifty to sixty postdoctoral fellows trained in my laboratory, all have returned to their countries."

A majority of the NIH scientists professed ignorance about the potential implications for U.S. labor policy of the presence of foreign scientists at NIH. Those who presented an opinion did so within the narrow confines of the institution. From this vantage point they concluded that there were no significant consequences. The following statements by two staff scientists are illustrative of the general view of the implications of the presence of foreigners at NIH for immigration and labor policies:

Not very much. These are mainly temporary positions. Movement into tenure track positions is absolutely minimal and requires U.S. citizenship. For example, the National Cancer Institute is now reviewing the applications of six candidates for such a slot. Of these, four are American, and two are foreign, and it is most likely that one of the Americans will be selected. In my 20 years of experience at NIH, I know of only one foreign scientist who got such a position.

No real impact because of the way it's set up. Foreign scientists come with the understanding that they are on visitor visas and are expected to return at the end of their tenure. Some persons get extensions. The Fogarty Center determines what can and cannot be done. In one case recently, an Australian scientist was offered an administrative position, but did not get an extension of visa and had to return home.

For those few interviewees who approached the matter from a broader labor market perspective, the implications were either nonexistent (not a real problem for highly skilled Americans because the number of likely skilled foreigners is small) or quite limited because unemployment rates among biomedical scientists (although not necessarily underemployment rates) are quite low. For one, at least, the issue was as much a foreign policy concern as a domestic labor policy matter. For this lab chief, "the Tiananmen Square incident is the best example . . . it shows how foreign policy has a definite effect on foreigners coming and looking to stay in America." This was when many of the Chinese scientists managed to adjust from temporary student or work visas to permanent status on the heels of the amnesty offered by the administration of President Bush following the 1989 student crackdown and Tiananmen Square massacre.

The assessments of former NIH administrators and scientists regarding the implications for U.S. immigration and labor policies were inconclusive. Some felt that even under the more restrictive conditions, potential immigrants and their prospective employers have a way of getting around rules and regulations. Ongoing immigration of scientists can only serve to maintain standards of scientific excellence with intensified labor market competition, they maintained. One commentator even concluded that continued immigration of foreign scientists brings some unexpected benefits by improving equal access for everyone. He reasoned that since many foreign nationals are visibly different from European-Americans and appear more like some American ethnic and racial minorities, they help promote a more level playing field. That is, their presence creates pressure to make equal access a reality. This view stands in stark contrast with the notion that skilled immigration does more harm than good to disadvantaged American minorities.

Current NIH American trainees generally took a balanced position regarding immigration and labor realities and federal policies. One of them addressed the matter by noting that it all depends on the perspective from which the situation is viewed. Employers may desire an abundant supply of U.S. and foreign scientific labor, whereas American scientists may be more concerned about the impact of additional researchers on their own employment prospects.

Former NIH American trainees expressed no need for changes in U.S. immigration and labor policies. The following remark was typical:

> I assume because it is such a small pool of a total amount of U.S. immigration that it is irrelevant . . . I am not sure it's a problem because biotechnology industry has created such a large number of jobs.

Moreover, as another put it,

> These folks have to jump through a lot of hoops to stay here. It's a long, expensive process. They need sponsors [in order] to stay, and the sponsors have to pay money for lawyers. The process is certainly not too lax.

One former NIH postdoc who is now on the staff of a research institute in California summed up the situation in this manner:

> Let's face it: Science is hard, dirty work. It can be dangerous, too, given some of the chemicals we work with. Americans don't want to do it; they can make more doing something else. The many years of long hours and low pay are very hard on marriages and family life. As a result, there is a shortage of Americans in science. This creates a big opportunity for the international scientists, who fill the niches. This is the way it has always worked in this country. It is positive in general.

The majority of the current NIH foreign trainees interviewed indicated that they intend to remain in the United States if possible. Therefore, it was hardly surprising that they all voiced the conviction that the United States greatly benefits from the contributions of foreigners to the nation's scientific research and biotechnology. Indeed, some of their comments on U.S. immigration and labor policies reflected a keen self-interest, as when several suggested that immigration regulations should be eased to accommodate the requirements of immigrants' relatives to facilitate their permanent settlement.

In general, the foreign scientists were of the opinion that current immigration policies "work well for NIH." Some pointed out that NIH's leadership can help exceptional scientists adjust their immigration status and that NIH constantly lobbies the U.S. Congress to make the J–1 visa more user-friendly. However, they also noted that NIH is not the easiest place to be for foreign postdoctoral trainees wishing to adjust status to either a temporary or a permanent work visa. "It is getting harder to get an H–1B visa," said one foreign postdoc, "but it is still not difficult to get a J–1." Many foreign trainees expressed frustration with the INS. They saw it as a regulatory agency intent on making their lives difficult should they try to remain in the United States. They were aware that J–1 visa holders are not eligible to apply for a permanent visa, and many understood the particulars of the H–1B visa very well.

In terms of employment policy, a fair number of the foreign postdocs felt that NIH's foreign trainee programs play a beneficial labor policy role for the United States mostly because foreign scientists are invited to the Bethesda campus to do work for which there are not sufficient American scientists available. They also firmly believed that if many of the foreign postdocs manage to get academic or industry jobs and remain in the United States, the end result will be good for America. A French immunologist saw the matter in relatively straightforward terms: "In the short term it is difficult and you hear that foreigners are stealing Americans' jobs, but in the long run it makes America better in science." Others took a more critical stance and observed that it is not in the best interest of any country to be as dependent on foreigners as is the United States on biomedical scientists from abroad. Some insisted that the United States should take a hard look at the situation and encourage more Americans to pursue rigorous science studies.

Another common opinion was that the labor market impact of the NIH foreign scientist training programs is nearly negligible since the total number of persons involved is insignificant in relation to the size of the U.S. labor market. The effect is, at worst, "neutral." Some pointed out that it was obvious that if NIH did not need foreign scientists, it would not be inviting so many of them to come.

A few former NIH foreign trainees who had returned home claimed they were unaware of potential problems in these areas, and a substantial majority was emphatic that there were no major immigration or labor policy implications. Some felt that the U.S. government maintains a tight grip on skilled immigration levels and limits competition for the jobs foreign biomedical scientists can engage in. A few alluded to potentially adverse effects, but they did not consider them to be significant.

Representative comments illustrate the most important points noted. One person, for example, to explain why she felt there were no detrimental migration consequences, indicated that INS very carefully regulates the immigration status of foreign scientists and, in any case, "the demand for biomedical scientists is so great that foreign scientists do not represent a competitive threat for American scientists." Another noted that undocumented immigration is not an issue among highly skilled scientists, adding that "if a foreign scientist manages to obtain an academic or industry position, it is very easy to obtain legal papers, often with the employer's assistance. The only thing that interferes is the scientist's personal capabilities." In fact, what NIH knows about foreign scientists, noted another, can be regarded as an excellent mechanism to draw the best foreign scientists to the United States from abroad. That is, the process is intended to actually facilitate skilled immigration. In this scientist's opinion, the competitive advantage the United States currently has in the biotechnology field is a result of the dynamics created by interactions among the best U.S. and foreign scientists.

Many foreign scientists recognized that a stint at NIH may open the door for those who want to stay in the United States, although they assumed that if foreigners remain, they must accept positions that American scientists as a rule do not want, such as a faculty post in the less prestigious U.S. universities. One saw the matter in dramatic terms: "The great influx of foreign scientists leads to savage competition: That is the reason why many people do not want to stay." However, he concluded that during prosperous times even a permanent labor market presence of foreign scientists might not be of any consequence, although in a recession the opposite could well be true. As one foreign scientist said, "It is complicated. You have to assess the harm perceived by a U.S. scientist who is by-passed in favor of a foreign scientist. You must also consider that few Americans want to go into basic sciences, something particularly true among M.D. s."

Former NIH foreign trainees remaining in the United States were of divided opinion regarding the implications that the presence of foreign scientists at NIH may have for U.S. immigration policy. A common view was that NIH has a great deal of influence with INS and thus the flow of foreign scientists can be easily manipulated, depending on the economic circumstances of the moment. Whenever it is convenient to the institution, NIH can intervene to address its concerns. One individual cited the case of a Russian scientist who was granted permanent resident status after making an important finding in cancer research. Others felt that with current immigration law, it is relatively difficult for foreign scientists to remain permanently in the United States. Conditions of work for foreign postdoctoral trainees are tightly regulated, and relatively few get hired on a permanent basis by NIH. However, as indicated by another Russian scientist with a permanent immigration visa currently employed at NIH who first came with a J–1 visa, NIH often acts as a back door to the American labor market. In his words,

> NIH has strict policies and hires such a small percentage [of foreign postdoctoral trainees]. But, if you get into NIH, there is a good chance you will be hired elsewhere. But at the same time, it is hard to stay at NIH because of NIH's visa requirements.

The implication, also voiced by others, is that since the demand for biomedical scientists in the American economy is currently so substantial that it is of no consequence whether NIH applies immigration regulations liberally or restrictively. Private sector firms, as well as universities, are often ready to offer them employment, either as permanent employees or postdoctoral researchers.

In regard to U.S. labor policy, some assumed that there would not be an impact within NIH itself, while others felt that the implications were nil largely because there is considerable demand for foreign biomedical scientists due to the perceived scarcity of American scientists. Their general feelings about the current situation wherein so many foreign biomedical scientists come to the United States and choose to stay was that it might be good for science in the long term because the United States has access to the best scientists. However, it was noted, there is a price to pay in the short run since the labor market might become saturated due to the growing size of a large competitive pool created by immigrants. Hence, it would be in the best interest of the United States to encourage more Americans to pursue scientific careers by doing something about the culture of commercialism in America that dissuades so many from doing so for fear of forfeiting high economic status.

Summary

Relatively few interviewees established direct connections between the presence of foreign biomedical science trainees at NIH and immigration and labor policies.

The most common view was that since the terms and conditions for the temporary presence of foreign trainees are so tightly regulated there are no apparent labor market implications.

A few parted company from this perspective and saw immigration regulations as largely ineffectual. For them,

- Regulatory safeguards can easily be overcome, and most foreign trainees wishing to remain in the United States manage to do so.

Many, however, did not see the ability of foreign scientists and their employers to manipulate the rules as detrimental to U.S. interests because foreign scientists contribute much to America's biomedical knowledge and economy. A related view was that

- The permanent settlement of foreign scientists in the United States is inconsequential, if not beneficial, given their specialized, skilled background and very limited numbers.

A small minority was worried about the present situation. For them, the relative ease with which foreign students and postdoctoral trainees manage to adjust visa status is a concern.

- The growing presence of foreign scientists adversely affects the interests of American scientists and may discourage U.S. students from pursuing careers in the biomedical sciences.

Notes

1. Appendix A summarizes verbatim information obtained from the National Institutes of Health webpage regarding foreign scientists training categories, stipends and salary schedules and other conditions of appointment, eligibility criteria, and visa requirements regarding visiting program options for all of NIH or selected institutes as of 1998. However, after fieldwork for the study was completed, NIH revised these categories (see Appendix E: New Intramural Professional Designations Introduced by NIH in 1999).
2. A verbatim summary of the types of visas available to foreign scientists at NIH culled from various sources is provided in Appendix C.
3. These are foreign research physicians that in order to have "full patient contact, and to receive credit for medical specialty board certification . . . must conduct their research under a J-1 visa sponsored by the Educational Commission for Foreign Medical Graduates (ECFMG) in those programs at NIH that meet graduate medical education or training accreditation standards."

4

Other Perspectives

This chapter presents perspectives gathered through interviews with representatives of biomedical communities in academe and industry that although not directly associated with NIH, nonetheless maintain close institutional collaborative research relations with or receive funding from NIH. Among those interviewed were U.S. university biomedical faculty and American and foreign graduate science students, as well as representatives of biomedical associations and of biotechnology firms. The views of these individuals complement those of persons who have been directly linked to NIH and add further dimensions to the understanding of NIH's role in biomedical research, globalization and international migration.

The View from Academia

During the course of this study, interviews were conducted with university biomedical faculty and graduate science students, both American and foreign, at selected universities. The perceptions reported here were derived primarily from interviews at a leading southern university known for its health-related academic programs, as well as from interviews with faculty and students from several Midwest, Eastern Seaboard, and West Coast universities. The purpose of the faculty interviews was to gain an appreciation of the extent to which the presence of foreign biomedical scientists in the United States is influenced by institutional relationships between NIH and the universities. Another objective was to assess faculty views regarding present trends in American biomedical education, including the training of U.S. and foreign students. Graduate student interviews were intended to shed light on whether and to what degree American and foreign doctoral students differ, to assess future postdoctoral and career plans, and, specifically, how NIH fits into those plans, if at all.

Biomedical Faculty

Biomedical university faculty members often alluded to how dependent their respective departments were on NIH for support, in some cases relying on NIH for as much as 75 to 80 percent of their funding. Most of this money comes in the form of research (or RO1) grants, which can be used to support the work of both American and foreign trainees. Also, American (but not foreign) trainees are eligible for individual National Research Science Award training grants. This reliance on and frequent faculty contact with personnel at the NIH Bethesda campus (when submitting proposals, as proposal readers, and as members of scientific review panels), together with relationships established through professional associations and scientific meetings, help forge strong links between intramural biomedical scientists and the extramural research community. These connections play an essential role in informing potential postdoctoral trainees of the availability of fellowship appointments at NIH and also act as vehicles through which recruitment for more permanent positions is channeled, whether to academe or industry. It is through these information pipelines that doctoral students make career choices, including evaluating options for postdoctoral training.

Faculty members stressed that a major reason why American institutions of higher education bring in foreign trainees—including undergraduate, graduate, and postdoctoral trainees—is because there are not enough qualified Americans coming through the educational system to fill available biomedical science positions. U.S. students, university faculty stated, are not studying the "hard" sciences as much as they used to, and, even when they do, it is often to pursue careers in medicine rather than in biomedical science. An often-expressed explanation for this phenomenon was that Americans do not want to do the hard work involved in science and that those who attend graduate school tend to study business, law, and medicine in preparation for more lucrative careers in these fields. In this vein, a professor of biology in a mid-Atlantic university offered these observations:

American BA graduates are not pursuing graduate study in the sciences. The graduate program in biostatistics at [our university] cannot continue to function without foreign students. Out of the 30 students we have in our Ph.D. program, only five are American. Americans are just not applying. That is the situation in the academic department; and here in our biostatistics center, out of the scientists with their Ph.D., almost all of them are foreign. The reason for this is because most new [American] Ph.D.s want a tenure track position and would prefer to stay in their postdoctoral position until they secure one. Americans turn down jobs here because they are not tenure-track positions. But in some cases the foreigner [is] the best person for the job.

Faculty members often stated that their institutions do not recruit per se, but their descriptions of efforts to announce the availability of funded graduate and postgraduate level positions seemed very vigorous and encompassed advertising in journals, communication through computer websites, and interactions at scientific meetings. They claimed to receive many applications from foreign trainees, especially Indians, Pakistanis, and Chinese from the People's Republic, who use what is characterized as a "shotgun approach": They apply for a great many positions in the hope of securing one—somewhere—just to establish a toe-hold in this country, and once they have arrived and learned their way around, they often move to other training institutions for various reasons, such as greater prestige, more ample financial support, or proximity to family members or friends. This practice of foreign trainees leaving institutions without giving notice was a source of complaint for a number of faculty, who viewed it as odd or disloyal. At any rate, all of the faculty members spoke of the high proportion of foreign trainees in their labs and departments. A member of a mid-Atlantic university chemistry faculty emphasized the degree to which his and other U.S. educational institutions, like NIH, have become dependent on foreigners for both trainees and instructors:

I think NIH is very much like U.S. universities in that they must try to "keep the show going." Universities need graduate students to have a graduate program and look competitive and respectable. In fact, out of the last 75 graduate students in [our university's] chemistry department, two were American. Most of our graduate students are either Chinese or Russian—but, like I said, you have to accept whatever you get to keep the show going and look good to the outside. I am sure the best schools . . . have made the least changes while lesser schools . . . have experienced massive change. Another factor is that many of the professors right now are first generation foreign-born immigrants who trained in the U.S. They have a direct pipeline to their countries and are at least as comfortable if not more comfortable advising foreign students. I think you would have to go back to 1970 to see a time when American chemistry graduate students outnumbered foreign chemistry graduate students.

A number of faculty members pointed out that the math and science training in foreign educational systems is superior to that in the United States at the secondary school and undergraduate levels. Also, it was noted that in U.S. universities, foreign students at all levels tend to cluster in the fields of biology, chemistry, and physics rather than in the arts and humanities, like their American counterparts. Further, frequent reference was made to the higher scores attained by foreign trainees, especially Asians, on the math and science portions of such standardized tests as the GRE and MCAT (Medical Comprehensive Aptitude Test).

Some U.S. university faculty informants felt that foreigners were generally better trained, although students from certain countries were less so. However, most faculty seemed to believe that the educational backgrounds and skills of foreign and U.S. trainees were comparable. It was noted that foreign trainees come with varying levels of skill in English, and that foreigners who lack fluency could work only as research assistants, while Americans could serve as either research assistants or teaching assistants. One area in which faculty tended to agree there is a major difference is in the foreigners' greater intensity of focus, motivation, and willingness to work hard, especially among Asians. A medical school faculty member whose extensive experience included many years as a lab chief at NIH put it this way:

> These foreign postdocs come with good training, are strong in the basic sciences, and speak English. The Japanese are especially skilled in certain areas, particularly in regard to precise, repetitive procedures. The foreign postdocs are willing to work 14 to 16 hours a day; they are the "workhorses" of the operation.

In the main, university professors believed that foreigners who complete their training and do not then return to their home countries represent competition for their U.S. counterparts. However, they varied in their interpretations of the loci and degrees of this competition.

For example, none thought that foreign scientists are a serious threat to Americans in terms of employment in the academy. They noted that tenured academic positions are now very hard to come by for anyone, but that, as a rule, U.S. science graduates would have the advantage over foreigners in securing such a job for a combination of reasons. These would include fluent English language speaking and writing skills, familiarity with American culture, greater knowledge of and ability to network within the U.S. biomedical professional system, and easier adaptation to the grant-writing and fund-raising processes required of faculty members.

A number felt that the biotechnology industry is now the source of greatest opportunities and competition for Americans and foreigners alike. A New England university biologist put it this way:

Right now it is quite open and exciting. Throughout the '80s a lot of people were under the misconception that if they couldn't get a job in academia they would [have to] go into industry. But the reality is that industry is very competitive as well. It's a personal choice of career path. One-third of our department's postdocs go into biotechnology—applied science. Twenty percent of our Ph.D.s get their postdoc and then go into the biotechnology industry. This department has a lot of M.A. students who are currently aligned with biotechnology companies that are paying for them to get their M.A.s.

Many perceived the competition provided by foreign scientists as a necessary phase in the generation of greater employment opportunities for all. In the words of a naturalized (Chinese-born) faculty member at a West Coast university, "On one end, it creates more competition; on the other end, it pushes U.S. science ahead and therefore expands employment and creates more jobs."

However, not all were quite so sanguine about what competition from foreigners means for the current and future employment prospects of American scientists. A Midwestern medical school lab chief gave this rather grim assessment:

The "local" level problem is displacing Americans. Labs claim they cannot find qualified Americans. Instead, they hire scientists from countries with lesser opportunities. They are highly motivated, more malleable, and demand less money. Of course employers want them—it keeps labor costs down. It is easier and cheaper [for employers] to exclude Americans in the short run, and there is no incentive to change the system. People don't seem to see that it will lead to long-term problems that will limit opportunities for their own children.

Many faculty members expressed dismay about the current trend in universities wherein fewer Americans are enrolling in biomedical studies while the number of foreigners is mushrooming. A few of these professors indicated that a major reason for this development lies at the feet of deans of academic departments who insist on perpetuating their "fiefdoms." They do this in two ways: maintaining large enrollments regardless of the quality of applicants, and depending on graduate students to serve as inexpensive research and training assistants. One medical school physician was particularly troubled by this widespread practice:

> It starts at the graduate school level by using graduate students as cheap labor who are retained as postdocs. Faculty claim they have trouble getting American graduate students, but they have neglected their responsibilities to American society by not making major efforts to improve the situation and recruit Americans. Actually, this problem starts below undergraduates. When it is easier to hire someone from another country than to improve and maintain your educational system, your society is in deep trouble and therefore science will eventually go elsewhere.

It was pointed out that another aspect of this problem is that training institutions apparently make these enrollment and training decisions without taking job market conditions into account, without evaluating supply and demand, and without looking to the future. That is, they do not appear to anticipate the shape of the job market by the time their graduates begin to look for work. Furthermore, they are oblivious to the need to prepare students for future employment contingencies. In the boom times of the late 1990s, people seemed to have forgotten the recession-induced downsizing of a few years earlier and the cyclical nature of economic activity. Moreover, the process of globalization and the burgeoning of the American biotechnology industry do not necessarily mean that everything will work to the advantage of American scientists. A professor and former dean of chemistry at a New England university offered these observations:

> That more and more R&D activities are being shipped abroad is raising concern as well. This is largely inevitable due to the globalization of the economy. More and more U.S. firms are being controlled by foreign cor-

porations. Although these corporations try to maintain a balance, what usually happens is that the balance shifts away from "our side of the pond." Another contributing factor is that R&D costs are usually lower abroad, and not only because of higher salaries here. Finally, as domestic corporations attempt to increase their foreign markets, they must shift some R&D activities abroad to better serve these markets.

A number of faculty members faulted NIH's Extramural Research Program for placing undue emphasis on research productivity rather than on research training, complaining that "powerhouse" institutions receive all the funding, and less productive undergraduate labs lose out. Instead, they argued, to find effective ways to interest American students in science and to attract them to biomedical research careers, NIH should take the lead by providing funding and guidelines for training students. The following comments by a New England university biology professor reflect the thoughts of many of her colleagues:

I think our concern about the U.S. present competitive position is getting in the way of what should be our main concern: How can the U.S. educational system ensure that we continue to train and produce highly skilled American students who can compete in the international scientific workforce? I think that the only way we can ensure adequate training for American students is if training institutions . . . receive money from federal agencies such as NIH. As it is now, NIH rewards productivity, not training. NIH needs to establish a division much like the Howard Hughes Foundation undergraduate initiative which gives undergraduate students money to do real research. There usually isn't enough money to go around to allow undergraduates to do basic research and as a result they have to wait to get that training at grad school. Meanwhile undergraduates in other countries are doing basic research and are ahead of the American undergraduates when applying to Ph.D. programs in America. The question NIH has to ask is whether training is part of productivity. The problem is, it is hard for an [training] institution to go against what is being rewarded which is not training but productivity. NIH has to figure out how to reverse the trend which is created by the process of NIH proposals.

University faculty tended to view bringing in foreign trainees as positive in creating a diverse learning environment. Also, they generally felt that graduate foreign scientists help enhance the international competitiveness of the United States. One Chinese-American professor actually felt that the contributions of foreigners are crucial to the success of the American scientific endeavor: "Foreigners have made America the best, particularly in the field of biomedicine. Foreigners have done this mostly by creating more competition." None of the university faculty believed that bringing foreign trainees and scientists to this country bears any immigration or labor policy implications that require correction.

Summary

Many faculty members felt that biomedical departments at U.S. universities are in a quandary since they must enroll foreign students in order to function. This is because there is:

- A dearth of qualified U.S. applicants primarily because fewer and fewer American students are choosing to pursue graduate studies in the natural sciences.
- An abundance of foreign applicants, many from countries that do better than the United States in providing undergraduate scientific training.

A good many faculty faulted the United States for being short-sighted regarding the training of young scientists and were especially critical of university departments that give priority to their interests rather than to those of their students.

- NIH is partly to blame because funding decisions for its grants emphasize research output rather than training.

Regardless of these concerns, however,

- The faculty interviewees saw no adverse implications for American scientists arising from the presence of a limited number of foreign scientists in the U.S. labor market.

Biomedical Graduate Students

The graduate education of several of the doctoral candidates interviewed was being partially supported by NIH training grants. Their views were highly consistent with those amply popularized in the press and also provided by other categories of interviewees as described above, particularly with respect to trainees of Asian origin.

The latter were portrayed as extremely committed and dedicated to their academic pursuits.

American biomedical graduate students consistently reported that whereas foreign students have a comparable level of training to American students, the former are generally more motivated than the latter. Most foreign students seemed to be much more focused and determined to complete their studies. As one American student commented, "they are more 'tunneled' in their work behavior. They seem more dedicated in some ways. They know where they're going and what they want to do." Foreign students were reported to be more willing "to give up their lives." They were characterized as always the first people to arrive at work in the morning and the last ones to leave, whereas Americans were not as willing to do that. In some cases, foreign students were said to be less prepared academically than American students, but that more often than not they managed to quickly catch up.

Foreign graduate students were reported as likely to spend more time in the lab. This tendency was attributed, according to American trainees, to the fact that foreign students feel more at home in the lab given that they come from a different culture and speak a different language. That is, the lab may be the most familiar, comfortable environment for them on the campus. Their academic backgrounds often differ as well since they are the products of different school systems. It was felt that the most frequent problem encountered by foreign trainees is the English language, which for many is a major hurdle.

One American stated that he had never known a foreign student with less skills or motivations than a U.S. national. It was generally agreed that foreign trainees' skills and personal attributes are largely determined by the part of the world they come from. Asians were identified as the most motivated and determined.

The U.S. university foreign biomedical trainees confessed to having difficulties in making generalizations about differences between foreign and U.S. biomedical trainees. In fact, there was a strong correspondence between the views of foreign and U.S. trainees in two important respects: In terms of scientific background, foreign and U.S. students do not differ much, whereas the former stand out in terms of motivations and work habits. The two groups, not surprisingly, also mentioned that many of the foreigners have difficulty with the English language, although some noted that in the international language of science there are no significant communication barriers.

Several foreign students pointed out that there are some significant differences in how scientific training is approached in the United States and other countries. In foreign countries, a twenty-seven-year-old Chinese male noted, foreign students tend to receive more training in theory and "more traditional training," in contrast to students in the United States where emphasis is placed on the use of the latest technologies. This leads to an interesting paradox in that although foreign students reputedly better understand the theories behind the application of the various technologies, they are not as familiar with their use. This situation is one of complementarity, continued the student, since foreign students can learn from the Americans how to use the techniques, whereas the Americans can gain insight from the theoretical understanding of the foreigners. Another foreign graduate student, also from China, identified another area in which foreign and American scientists complement each other: American biomedical students are as a rule more creative, an approach foreign students should imitate. American students, on the other hand, should learn to be more hard working.

Differential motivation was explained in terms of various factors. Several, including an Indian national, mentioned that foreign students are more motivated simply because they have to overcome many hurdles in order to enroll in an American university. Another reason why foreign students work harder and for longer hours, offered by a Czech student, is that they "don't have a social life." An Australian enrolled at an elite northeastern university felt, however, "that every one works so hard that it is hard to tell them apart. Most Americans are not from Boston. Therefore, they, like the foreigners, do not have their family here. So there is not much difference." A thirty-three-year-old Chinese student accounted for the foreigners' dedication to work by referring to a lack of social and communication skills, areas in which Americans excel, at least in the United States. A couple of foreign students commented, however, that in reality foreigners and Americans are not that different regarding motivation. American students, it was noted, have a lot of freedom to choose; if they choose to go into biomedical science, a very difficult field of study, they must be sufficiently motivated. Several foreign students commented that the deep motivation of foreign scientists, as well as their greater productivity in the United

States, could be attributed, at least in part, to the greater availability of resources and financial support they receive while at American campuses.

Some of the foreign students concurred with the views expressed by Americans that more often than not, the former have better-defined academic and training objectives than the latter. An Irish interviewee indicated that Americans, as a rule, are more uncertain of what they ultimately want to do, and they keep exploring different alternatives.

Among the American biological science students interviewed, most planned to exclusively consider pursuing postdoctoral training positions at academic institutions, whereas some were willing to apply for such appointments at either universities or government research institutions, such as NIH or the Centers for Disease Control and Prevention. Yet, several said they were interested solely in applying for postdoctoral positions or jobs with private industry. Most U.S. students hoped to have an academic career, except for those with their sights fixed on private industry. Despite the fact that most were aware of the difficulty of gaining an academic appointment, they explained that this was their objective. Many noted that universities do not prepare students for a professional life beyond the confines of academe. One commented that at his university the faculty seemed oblivious to the reality that most doctoral students will not end up as tenured academic researchers.

Some of the American biomedical students said they would be willing to consider a NIH postdoc since it could provide them with insights as to how the biomedical research bureaucracy works. Several felt that a training fellowship at NIH would presumably help them understand how to prepare a grant proposal. This reasoning revealed a lack of familiarity with NIH at this stage of their training; many experienced researchers and advanced postdocs are against applying to NIH for a postdoctoral fellowship precisely because they are not exposed to, nor do they acquire, proposal writing skills in that setting. One graduate student considered a NIH postdoc as a highly desirable experience because he thought that the more stable jobs, aside from tenured academic appointments, depend on NIH grants. These students regarded NIH as an attractive postdoctoral option, viewing it as providing a congenial working environment, state-of-the-art equipment, and plentiful resources. A postdoctoral stint at NIH could be used, furthermore, to bridge the gap between academia and industry.

At the same time, doing a NIH postdoc was regarded as having several disadvantages. Those seeking teaching experience would not be happy there since NIH only offers postdoctoral research appointments with no teaching opportunities. One student was concerned about limited publishing opportunities at NIH due to patent issues, while others felt that as a government agency NIH has far too many regulations.

During the interviews, several American students addressed migration issues. One speculated that it might be easier for foreign students to receive NIH postdoctoral appointments based on his experience in one experimental course at his university in which the majority of students were foreigners. Another reached exactly the opposite conclusion and felt that most foreign scientists would not be interested in NIH because it offers lower stipends than other institutions. One student felt that the hiring of foreign scientists has the potential to harm U.S. international competitiveness in biotechnology because, he contended, contracts offered to foreigners generally undercut wages for U.S. scientists. This is shortsighted, the student said, "America needs to"'wake up' and upgrade education in the U.S., not rely on foreigners, to make the U.S. more competitive." This same student felt that current immigration regulations are far too liberal and that employers take advantage of them. The result is that wages for American workers, "skilled and unskilled, both foreigners and Americans," suffer. One female graduate student believed that most foreign biomedical students eventually plan to return to their home countries, although as a general rule they would like to complete their postdoctoral training in the United States.

Only a few of the foreign biomedical science students interviewed had a clear sense of the mission and programs of NIH. Actually, a surprisingly large proportion of them knew hardly anything about NIH, and some of those who claimed to have some understanding of the institution held erroneous notions. The opinion verbalized by one foreign biomedical student illustrated this vividly. He did not want to pursue postdoctoral training at NIH because it is an academic institution and he did not want to teach. This same European, however, was strongly inclined against remaining in the United States, which may explain his poor understanding of NIH's mission. Others were not likely to include NIH as a postdoctoral option because "positions there are not open to foreign students." Some interviewees saw NIH as primarily a funding source for university-based biomedical research programs, although a few were aware of its intramural research functions, as suggested by comments about "leading scientists in my field working there" and NIH's "high academic level and a good reputation."

All but one of the foreign students interviewed were already making postdoctoral training plans. Most were interested in finding postdoctoral fellowships in the United States, with only two, a European and an Australian, saying they were planning to return to their countries. Revealingly, of those foreign students planning to do postdoctoral training, most wanted to remain permanently in the United States. One noted that at his U.S. university, most foreign postdocs stay in the United States, with about half of those finding jobs in academia and the remainder in industry.

Summary

In general, American biomedical science graduate students seemed to be much better informed than foreign students about the mission of NIH and what a postdoctoral training appointment there entails, but even the former did not have a very clear view. This lack of familiarity may in part be explained by the point at which the students interviewed were in their careers, a reasonable assumption being that the closer they get to graduation, the more familiar they probably become with postdoctoral appointment options. The three most interesting points of information to emerge from these interviews were that:

- Most American science graduate students were interested in pursuing academic careers although they were well aware that university jobs are difficult to find.
- Most foreign graduate students wanted to remain in the United States permanently or at least for an extended period of time.
- Some American students were already troubled about their career prospects, had some familiarity with the assumed labor market consequences of the immigration of foreign scientists, and were concerned about the universities' inaction in preparing them for non-academic careers.

The View from Biomedical Associations

Representatives of professional biomedical associations were interviewed to gain their views regarding the issues involved in this study.

The reason for interviewing these individuals was to ascertain if they could provide insights not readily available through their organizations' official position papers.

From their perspectives, there are several reasons why American research institutions, including NIH, offer postdoctoral training opportunities to foreigners and recruit foreign scientists for temporary and permanent positions. Some of these reasons were related to perceived faults in U.S. training policies, such as not being well calibrated and at times not serving this country's long-term interest. Nonetheless, the dominant view was that it would be a major mistake, as stated by a representative of one of the leading national biomedical associations, for the U.S. federal government to implement laws and regulations that "interfere with Nobel price winners gaining entry to the United States." It is critical, he went on, to assure the continued and fluid movement of senior and junior scientists. Echoing this sentiment, another noted that if the immigration door were to be shut, the United States would be hurt. In the long run, he said, "the increased availability of foreign trained scientists increases job availability domestically."

Some explained that while shortages of biomedical scientists in specialized fields often occur, this has less to do with basic shortage/surplus issues per se than with the way that shortages develop. A number pointed out that the United States does not have a long-range, coherent plan for national health. Market forces always prevail. The same holds true for public-funded health science research in the United States: Abrupt shifts are made in response to politico-economic pressures, resulting in the "disease of the year syndrome." Examples of sudden swings away from previously prioritized research endeavors to politically hot research issues include Alzheimer's Disease and other diseases of the elderly, HIV/AIDS, and breast cancer. Because scientific training and research are by their very nature long-term endeavors, dislocations occur. This situation is aggravated by a tendency among some employers, including research institutions, to hire only "the best" and "most-up-to-date" in the world—that is, those requiring no further training—to serve the needs of the moment. In the view of one association representative,

> Because of an ample supply of foreign workers, U.S. industry can avoid having to retrain the domestic work force. Foreign worker availability also helps industry reduce costs. This occurs not because foreign workers re-

ceive lower salaries, but because an expanded skilled work force exerts a downward pressure on wages. Foreign workers also take the pressure off the government, since the government does not have to rely solely upon American resources to satisfy demand. In the absence of the foreign alternative, the government would be forced to devote more attention to domestic training. If this approach were to be followed, the growth of the non-technical pool of U.S. workers would be slowed down.

Some individuals took issue with the argument that an excessive number of scientists are being trained in the United States. They thought this interpretation to be erroneous because foreign scientists fill a void by joining the U.S. research infrastructure. One interviewee in particular offered several policy suggestions to enhance opportunities for U.S. scientists when large influxes of foreign scientists in specific fields are in evidence, especially when economic fluctuations impact on the demand for scientific talent. The government, for example, should consider establishing a moratorium on the hiring of foreign scientists when indicated by the stage of the economic cycle, and should also alert scientific societies about employment opportunities in particular fields as information accumulates regarding the influx of scientists in a particular field. Several taxation mechanisms were also mentioned as potentially effective policy tools. For example, those wishing to hire foreign scientists could be allowed to do so as long as they pay a tax designed to promote the scientific training of American students.

It was also noted in several of the interviews that most foreign scientists, like American scientists, prefer to go into academia, and, that for the last twenty-odd years, more and more graduate school slots have been occupied by foreigners. Also, a process of credential creep to achieve desirable employment positions has been underway for the last two decades. This has been manifested in an increase in the number of years that science Ph.D.s must currently commit to postdoctoral positions. A two-year postdoc is now considered essential since this practical training serves to build basic wet bench skills to complement academic and graduate training. The normal path today is to spend four years on average in postdoctoral positions. Those who spend more time than that do so for career reasons (the desire to acquire additional skills in the highly complex and interdisciplinary scientific biomedical environment or to make themselves more employable). Others do so because they have no other choice in terms of finding permanent career employment. Postdocs in NIH's Intramural Research Program are in positions comparable to those funded in universities through NIH's Extramural Research Program.

The issue of U.S. international competitiveness and the presence of foreign scientists in the U.S. labor force was viewed by biomedical and biotechnology association representatives as complex. The consensus was that this country gains through the presence of foreign scientists. The U.S. government encourages investments in science by financing research programs at NIH and elsewhere. The knowledge thus gained becomes part of the national patrimony. The problem is that access to this national patrimony cannot be controlled, and benefits deriving from it are not exclusive. However, although borders are permeable, they are not completely fluid. There is considerable evidence, noted one person, that suggests that locally generated know-how is retained since scientific advancement depends to some extent on a country's ability to generate knowledge. If this is in fact the case, to the extent that "foreign scholars and students work here and contribute to the generation of local knowledge, the United States is enriched by the experience. The United States is so far ahead of the rest of the world in biomedical science that competition doesn't matter. The idea of technology leakage to other countries has been grossly overestimated."

As for the implications of foreign scientist immigration for U.S. labor policy, most of the association representatives felt that they were inconsequential or at worst modest. One argument used to reach this conclusion was that fewer young Americans are entering the hard science fields. Shifting priorities and the irregularity of research funding, according to several individuals, cause Americans to not select research scientist careers. Although scientists do not expect to make a lot of money upon completing their education, they do place a high value on job stability and financial security. Further, the status of research scientist is not highly valued in the United States, especially in comparison to those of physicians, lawyers, and business school graduates, whose training periods are shorter and are more likely to lead to wealth, power, and prestige. The comparative perspective provided by a naturalized English-born scientist who is a former NIH trainee and is now affiliated with a U.S. professional association is particularly instructive:

Science students in the British Commonwealth nations and other countries (e.g., France, Germany, Japan) are as a rule selected for higher education at an early age, undergo rigorous training in the basic sciences over an extended period of time, and often have their education subsidized by their governments. Also, attainment of a Ph.D. is prestigious in these societies. Because of job limitations at home, foreign scientists are eager to pursue training and careers in the U.S. that hold the potential for greater long-term opportunities. These foreign students/workers thus have a background in hard work, take the long view, and are willing to do what they must to achieve these opportunities. Ironically, they can often obtain training support from U.S. agencies that is at times unavailable to U.S. citizens. For example, the Fogarty Fellowships were until a few years ago restricted to foreign students, but in acknowledgment of complaints of unfairness, the grant program was extended to include Americans. It is interesting to note, however, that the level of support rose from $18,000 to $26,000 per trainee.

This underscores the point, in the view of several interviewees, that the United States can always attract well-trained foreign students and professionals who are more than willing to accept less pay in the short run to gain long-term career opportunities they might not have in their countries of origin. Foreign postdoctoral students, just like U.S. postdocs, are often paid less than technicians. In addition, as one individual commented, foreign workers with temporary visas are malleable due to their "indentured servant" employment and residence status in the United States. But even after they have gained the status of permanent resident, they are still more likely than U.S. workers to accept less: In many of their home countries, almost any offer is a good offer, salary ranges are narrow, and "haggling" is not practiced.

One person noted that some concern exists among members of scientific associations about the qualifications of postdocs from certain countries that come to the United States with sub-standard credentials. There is a growing perception that some of the less prestigious schools may be "becoming sweatshops for foreign postdocs." Another association representative made the "off the record comment" that some foreign scientists are hired "because they are willing to work for less."

Summary

While interviews were in general congruent with the official views of the leading biomedical professional associations, several additional perspective were offered.

- One of the reasons driving the growing influx of foreign biomedical scientists is that, as a nation, the United States does not have a coherent, long-term health care plan. Biomedical research goals are established not on the basis of scientific merit, but rather of political and social pressures. This leads to the setting of short-term and unattainable research objectives for which there never is an adequate supply of appropriately qualified scientific personnel.
- The federal government should regulate the influx of foreign scientists in unison with fluctuations in labor demand arising from the economic cycle and in accordance with labor market data regarding the needed mix of specific skills.
- Since the supply of foreign biomedical scientists is elastic and they are willing to accept lower salaries in the short term to satisfy long-term career objectives, U.S. employers can avoid having to pay higher salaries and to upgrade the skills of the domestic scientific workforce.
- There is concern that in some of the less prestigious academic institutions foreign postdocs with substandard credentials from certain countries may be in the process of becoming a scientific underclass.

The View from the Biotechnology Industry

At the time this study was begun in 1997, it was deemed essential to gather information from representatives of biotechnology firms since it is known that this industry is a major employer of both American and foreign biomedical scientists. We were primarily interested in gaining some understanding of how these firms recruit their scientific research staff, why these firms employ foreign scientists, how much are they willing to invest to hire foreign scientists, and what role NIH plays, if any, in their recruitment strategy.

According to the information gathered, it appears that biotechnology firms employ research scientists from practically every major biological specialty, including molecular biology, biochemistry, cell biology, immunology, and virology. As biotechnology applications increasingly cut across traditional disciplinary lines, more and more firms are also hiring candidates with backgrounds in engineering, physics, computers, and other scientific fields. Applied research biotechnology firms hire first and foremost doctoral scientists, but most also employ individuals with masters and bachelors degrees. Some firms, however, regard a doctoral degree as essential.

One person associated with a large multinational firm noted that "you may hire someone with lesser skills than a Ph.D. with the intention to train him, but, at the end of the day, you find that it makes more sense to hire a newly minted Ph.D. since he brings to the table far more technical knowledge and skills." A representative of a firm working on a NIH genetic annotation contract made a similar observation by observing that her firm had decided to move away from employing scientists with less than a Ph.D. degree. She remarked that "Ph.D.s are necessary since they have the required background and level of sophistication to understand submission details and to raise technical issues with scientists forwarding submissions to the database."

The business focus and size of biotechnology companies accounts for the types of scientists employed, as does the rapid pace of scientific and technological development. Scientists of very diverse backgrounds work for large multinational firms in locations around the world. Smaller biotechnology firms, including start-up companies, tend to employ scientists with narrower backgrounds. Molecular biologists, for example, are not the employment focus of a firm concentrating on cancer diagnostics. This firm's employment priority would be Ph.D. scientists with a cytology background. Some firms address specific employment needs by establishing mentoring programs to integrate scientists with special skills into their research priority areas.

Recruitment

In the buoyant economic times of the late 1990s, biotechnology firms were constantly scanning the scientific employment marketplace and seeking the best available candidates. Standard recruitment practices utilized to identify professionals in the biotechnology industry are as common as in any other knowledge-driven field. Firms recruit scientists with specialized skills, as one individual put it, " because we can't afford to train our scientists: applicants either have the specialized training required or they are not hired."

Scientists employed by biotechnology companies are primarily but not exclusively recruited in universities. Most are hired after completing one or more postdoctoral appointment at universities, NIH, or private industry, while some are hired from among the faculty ranks of leading research universities, whether in the United States or abroad. Still others are lured away from other biotechnology companies. Recruitment patterns appear to be mediated by labor market conditions in particular scientific fields. A representative of one of the largest pharmaceutical firms in the world observed, for example, that "because of greater scarcity of chemists, brand new Ph.D. chemists tend to be recruited directly from universities, whereas biologists are usually recruited after they have had postdoctoral experience."

Some companies send recruitment letters to leading research universities, including foreign universities, if qualified U.S. scientists cannot be identified. Positions are posted in company-managed websites and ads placed in *Science* magazine and technical journals. Just as often recruitment is done by word of mouth and through employee referrals.

Some biotechnology firms depend heavily on educational and ethnic networks, whereas others shy away from these recruitment networks and prefer to rely on advertisements and professional headhunters. Typical of what biotechnology firms go through in the constant search for scientific personnel is the description below:

> The firm keeps a large file of resumes our representatives pick up at professional meetings, events like this job fair, and others they receive in the mail—some unsolicited and others in response to advertisements. When seeking to fill a position we often go to the resume file first. When advertising, we usually begin, as a local firm, with the *Washington Post*. We are aware that people across the United States consult the *Washington Post* for position announcements.

Recruitment booths are conspicuous at job fairs set at domestic and international scientific meetings where recruiters screen applicants. At the 1997 Annual Meeting of the American Society for Biochemistry and Molecular Biology—held in conjunction with the 17th International Congress of Biochemistry and Molecular Biology—in San Francisco, for example, members of our research team saw in action a sophisticated recruitment operation. Attended by thousands of participants from around the world, this conference included a career resource center run by the Federation of American Societies for Experimental Biology (FASEB), the umbrella association for biomedical scientists. It included a job placement service that scheduled on-site interviews between applicants and prospective private and public sector employers that also offered other services, such as career development workshops. During this week-long conference, employment interviews per prior appointment were held for three consecutive days from nine in the morning until five in the afternoon, as well as during the morning of a fourth day. While the majority of interviewing recruiters represented American universities, some were there on behalf of federal government agencies, including NIH and the Food and Drug Administration (FDA). Included among the more than seventy recruiting organizations were some of the leading global pharmaceutical and biotechnology companies, such as Brystol Myers Squibb, DuPont, Genentech, and Merck & Company. Brief conversations with many of the job seekers left the impression that foreign scientists dominated the ranks of the job applicants.

The same was true at other gatherings of biomedical scientists, including events expressly organized to facilitate labor market contacts, such as the annual NIH Job Fair. This less formal event is sponsored to introduce potential postdoctoral fellow candidates to universities, government agencies, or private sector firms recruiting scientists. At the 1997 and 1998 job fairs, for instance, there were recruiters from more than two dozen entities, including American and foreign multinationals such as the Bayer Corporation, Hoechst Marion Roussel, Johnson & Johnson, and BioWhittaker. At the 1998 fair there was a clear preponderance of foreign job seekers.

Biotechnology companies recruit scientists at NIH through informal channels, although we came across some companies that had no employees formerly associated with NIH. Company representatives differed significantly regarding the desirability of using NIH as a recruitment source for postdoctoral scientists. One industry representative claimed that NIH is an excellent recruiting ground and noted that all of his company's foreign scientists were former NIH postdoctoral fellows. "We have found," he added, "that NIH [foreign] postdocs come to the United States to look for university positions but are now testing the waters in private industry." He went on to say that at his firm, "all the foreigners are recruited through Fogarty."

Representatives of other biotechnology firms were far less enthusiastic about employing former NIH postdoctoral trainees. "It has been our experience," noted a representative of one of the leading biotechnology firms providing gene expression information to the pharmaceutical industry, "that NIH postdocs don't know how to serve people. They are good in terms of scientific background, but they sometimes have egos."

In summary, in good economic times biotechnology firms are constantly on the lookout for scientific talent. They are particularly eager to identify Ph.D. scientists with specialized skills. For some of these firms, job fairs held at NIH and at national and international scientific meetings offer particularly rich recruiting grounds. NIH's appeal as a recruitment location is that "in no other place in the world are there so many biomedical scientists under a single roof."

Reasons for Joining Biotechnology Firms

When asked why Ph.D. scientists join their firms, many biotechnology firm representatives gave responses that emphasized the good working conditions offered by their companies or the compatibility between the firm's research and development lines of inquiry and the professional and scientific interests of the Ph.D.s they recruit. Some firms touted their interdisciplinary environments and others highlighted their personnel benefits, while still others called attention to their leading research focus in the industry. Typical was the comment given by a representative of a growing biotechnology company that is engaged in the discovery of genes useful for the development of pharmaceutical, diagnostic, and proprietary database products. This firm claims to be "developing the products of the 21st Century. We offer competitive salaries and benefits and the opportunity for rapid professional growth. Scientists here get the best science around and the best working environment."

There are less positive reasons why scientists join a particular firm, as related by a young scientist acting as a recruiter for genetic annotators. According to her, at times scientists accept such positions because the employment market is very tough. She became an annotator after completing two sequential three-year postdoc appointments. After exhaustively searching she claimed to have applied for academic jobs at practically every American university; this was the only job she was able to land.

National Origin Composition of Foreign Scientists Employed by Biotechnology Firms

The national origin composition of the foreign scientists employed by the biotechnology firms contacted during the conduct of the study varied significantly. About the only major predictors of national origin diversity are company size and international projection, although some small firms, mostly oriented to the U.S. market, were staffed heavily by foreign-born biomedical scientists. All but one of the fourteen contacted firms had foreign-born scientists on staff. In most instances, foreign-born scientists had received at least some of their training in U. S. academic institutions. Foreign-born scientists working for these firms originated from all major regions of the world, but Asians (China, India, Pakistan) and Eastern Europeans, including Russians, appeared to be over-represented. Japanese and Western Europeans were often found as well.

A recruiter from one of the largest global pharmaceutical firms, with headquarters in Europe, stressed that the firm's scientific staff is recruited from all parts of the world. The national composition of the scientific staff at any one of the company's research labs (located in various countries) may be influenced by the country where the particular lab is located, but this is not a major criterion in selecting staff. As a global company, this multinational enterprise is not concerned about where its scientific staff comes from—in fact, "it does not matter." This view was common among representatives of other biotechnology firms, even among relatively small ones.

The perspective of a representative of just such a firm based in the Washington metropolitan area is especially interesting. The success and growth of his firm partly depends on the placement of its scientists in clients' laboratories, whether in the United States or abroad. This company could not be as successful if it did not have well-trained scientists familiar with other cultures and capable of speaking foreign languages. For this company, biotechnology operates in a global marketplace.

Comparison of Foreign and American Biomedical Scientists

In general, biotechnology firm representatives did not report appreciable differences in the knowledge and skills of U.S.-born and foreign scientists. The consensus was that these firms recruit from among the world's scientific elite where skill levels are nearly equally matched. Only those with the highest skills are recruited, regardless of nationality. As stated by a representative from one of these firms, technical expertise is the number one consideration in hiring. Secondary factors are demonstrated ability to work effectively in a U.S. setting and to communicate well in written and spoken English. Verbal skill was a consideration repeatedly emphasized, and where U.S. and foreign scientists were found—not surprisingly—to vary the most. Among U.S.-born scientists, interpersonal and communication skills are consistently high, but with foreign-born scientists they vary.

Foreign biomedical researchers cover the gamut of disciplines and specialties. The only demarcating factor that seems to separate them, according to a neuroscientist affiliated with a major American multinational pharmaceutical firm, is "that the foreigners are mainly involved in non-clinical research, and the Americans are involved in both basic and clinical research."

Some representatives noted that U.S. scientists possess more sophisticated business know-how, whereas foreign-born scientists have stronger scientific foundations, are better at mathematics, and have more of a hands-on attitude as scientists. It was also commented that domestic and foreign-born scientists tend to differ in some cultural dimensions. Scientists from some Asian countries, for example, were said to be more deferential and reticent about talking in meetings.

In discussing whether U.S. and foreign-born scientists differ in terms of attitudes and behavior, some individuals provided rather stereotypical opinions once they went beyond the most common claim of no differences. Many described foreign scientists as more intense and dedicated to their work. This was explained on the basis of several cultural reasons. It was believed, for example, that foreign scientists generally regard having a Ph.D. science degree as more prestigious than do Americans. Chinese and Indians were described as especially aware of social standing; they prized the Ph.D. They were prone to work hard in the United States because they value the opportunities encountered in the United States, as compared to the home countries where laboratories are poorly equipped. As one representative said, "They take advantage of the 'developed' setting." One felt Eastern Europeans to be more global in their approach to science and life, whereas American scientists are more narrow and specialized. U.S.

scientists were also widely held to be more liberal and to not like discipline, in contrast to more disciplined foreign scientists.

The prevailing view among representatives of the biotechnology industry was, therefore, that to the extent that foreign scientists manage to find their way into the United States, at NIH or elsewhere, whether as postdoctoral trainees or landed immigrants, they are comparable to Americans in terms of technical skills.

Sponsorship of Foreign Scientists

Most U.S. firms would much rather hire American scientists than foreigners to avoid the associated trouble and expense as long as U.S. scientists with comparable skills are available. This was an attitude consistently voiced by private sector representatives.

Most members of biotechnology firms stated that their companies are willing to sponsor foreign scientists for temporary or permanent work visas, and, in fact, many have done so. However, the vast majority stipulated that their firms are willing to do so primarily if the scientist in question matches a particular technical skill being sought. One person indicated, for example, that "if the individual has something special to offer in knowledge and skills, the company will go through the process because it will be considered cost effective." Yet another biotechnology firm representative remarked—after noting that it all depended on a foreign scientist's skills—that "if it is something we absolutely have to have, we will work with them, otherwise we will go somewhere else." We were struck during our interviews by how familiar some of the biotechnology firm representatives were with regard to the various types of work visas, such as the differences between an H–1B and a permanent residency certification.

Larger firms appeared to sponsor foreign scientists more frequently and to have well-developed infrastructures to handle these petitions, often through human resources departments. Identifying who bears the transaction costs of status adjustment seems to be dependent on how badly a firm needs the particular skills of a foreign scientist. In one representative's firm, the policy is guided by the individual's level of technical expertise. This determines "whether we would pay the entire cost or share costs."

International Competitiveness

Biotechnology firm representatives were uniform in their belief that U.S. international competitiveness in the industry gains from the presence of foreign scientists. As one said, "Having the best and brightest coming here is to America's advantage on the assumption that we retain them, of course." The latter is an important qualifier. "But if they come here, get trained, and then return to their own country," as the same person stated, "that leads to competition." On balance, however, it was generally held that the situation is probably pretty much a trade-off, with America getting the overall advantage since the United States scientific establishment probably learns and profits more from the presence of the foreign scientists than it loses from the knowledge developed here that they may take away.

Immigration and Labor Policies Implications

Biotechnology firm representatives did not see major ramifications for U.S. immigration and labor policies related to the employment of foreign biomedical scientists. The general assumption behind this conclusion is that there is demand for the services of foreign scientists, and that as long as that demand is there, there will be pressure from universities and industry to keep the immigration door open. Current immigration policies that grant preferential treatment to scientists are prone to remain unaltered because a much better case can be made for admitting the highly educated than the unskilled.

As far as potentially adverse labor market impacts, there will always be claims of the displacement of American by foreign scientists. As in everything else, several biotechnology firm representatives implied, there are always two sides to every story. It can be concluded that the general feeling among them was that during the prosperous late 1990s overall demand for highly skilled scientists in the biomedicine and biotechnology sectors was high, although certain types of jobs (e.g., in academia) were in short supply.

Summary

Based on our interviews with biotechnology firm representatives, several tentative conclusions can be reached. These appear to transcend firm size and to apply with equal vigor to U.S. and foreign-based pharmaceutical and biotechnology firms that operate internationally and that often have research and production facilities in different countries.

- These firms employ biomedical scientists from many backgrounds, but prioritize the hiring of those with specialized skills in emerging fields.
- Although the industry hires scientists at various levels of training, a doctoral degree is more often than not regarded as essential.
- Biotechnology firms are not overly concerned about national origins when recruiting. They focus on their requirements and on scientific skills.
- U.S.-based biotechnology firms, if necessary, are prepared to go through the effort and expense of sponsoring foreign scientists for residency in the United States.
- Biotechnology firms do not see any major immigration and labor policies implications arising from the employment of foreign scientists. Foreign scientists are perceived as being few in number and available to satisfy a demand for very specialized skills.

5

From the National Institutes of Health to the U.S. Labor Market

NIH Foreign Trainees:
Why They Come and Future Plans

There are many reasons why foreign postdocs come to NIH, but they are all associated, in one way or another, with the international networks linking scientists across the globe. The interviews provided a window to the increasing internationalization of biomedical education and postdoctoral research, as manifested in the cross-national nature of doctoral studies in the United States, as well as in European and Asian countries. Asians are as prone to study in Japan as are students from all over the world to choose European or North American universities for their education or to engage in postdoctoral training. Equally remarkable is the ease with which recent graduates are willing to go to another country to pursue postdoctoral training. These decisions are invariably influenced by the desire of young scientists to acquire international academic and research experiences to help advance their careers. This is true whether or not visiting young trainees eventually choose to stay in the countries where they receive training or decide to return to their home countries.

At NIH, in the United States, the decision is mediated by NIH-initiated recruitment efforts (through the international scientific literature, booths set at conferences, the Internet), referrals of young scientists to NIH staff by senior foreign scientists, and recommendations to NIH colleagues by U.S. faculty for foreign students enrolled at American universities. Many foreign scientists covet a NIH appointment given its international prestige, its clout in financing biomedical research, and its many research opportunities. A surprisingly large number of foreign scientists appear to find their way to NIH via the operation of ethnic networks that are increasingly recognized as powerful determinants of skilled migration and other less selective international labor migration flows. Many other candidates, aware of the well-publicized training opportunities available at NIH, apply for postdoctoral appointments on their own.

Examples of direct recruitment by current NIH staff were common in our interviews. A computational biologist from India, for example, described how after "a brief successful collaboration on a project with my current group leader [at NIH], I was called in for an interview and subsequently recruited." Several other interviewees related how an initial contact at an international conference led shortly thereafter to an invitation to come to NIH. The scope of these contacts is truly global, as described by scientists from Pakistan, England and Japan who were recruited at conferences held in their own countries.

A variant of this approach was described by a number of interviewees, who, through contacts with NIH scientists abroad, made known that they were interested in spending time at NIH and were then offered the opportunity to do so. A typical instance was described by a Ukrainian molecular biologist. While his university [in Ukraine] was conducting a joint research project with NIH, he was invited to work at the Bethesda campus for a two-month period. Since the experience was enjoyable, the young scientist approached his future boss and asked him to consider him for a postdoctoral appointment. The laboratory director agreed.

Personal relationships play an important function in channeling postdoctoral candidates to NIH. Often we came across interviewees who mentioned they had gone to NIH because of personal links between their national academic mentors and senior NIH colleagues. Not uncommon was the experience of a German female oncologist who described the circumstances that led to her NIH appointment. After her current laboratory chief gave a lecture in Germany, he asked a good friend of hers (working in the same research area) if "he knew of anyone he could hire as a postdoc, and he hired me." A Korean student noted that a professor in Japan suggested that NIH would be a good place for him to do a postdoc. After attending a lecture given by a NIH scientist in his hometown, an Argentinean biochemist contacted the NIH lecturer and through him was able to secure the financial support needed for a postdoc at Bethesda. In many countries, specialized institutes (such as the Consejo Nacionàl de Ciencia y Tecnología [CONACYT] in Argentina) assist their nationals to further their training at NIH by providing scholarships through existing international scientific collaborative programs.

Well-publicized NIH recruitment efforts and the international biomedical research programs it supports explain much of the success the institutes have in attracting promising young scientists to its campus. A German biologist applied for a NIH postdoc after he saw an advertisement in the journal *Science,* a reason echoed by a Chinese postdoc who stated: "I saw an add in a newspaper, applied and was accepted." Another interviewee, this time from Ukraine, noted that all young scientists know about NIH and the opportunities it offers "because that is where the money comes from." A French experimental immunologist expressed a similar sentiment when he noted that the "scientific community circles the globe. Everyone knows of NIH."

Finally, several of the interviewed postdocs indicated they had come to NIH thanks to the suggestions made by or through the auspices of friends from their own countries. This finding did not come as a complete surprise given the power of ethnic networks in international labor recruitment. Yet, we did not anticipate ethnic networks could be as prevalent in the recruitment of scientific talent as they appear to be given biomedical scientists' exceptionally high qualifications. During our interviews and observations at NIH, we were struck by how common it is for labs to be primarily staffed by postdocs from a common source country. These patterns clearly suggest that ethnic networking is an active, if informal, component of postdoctoral recruitment. The case of a molecular biologist from China can be used to illustrate this finding. As he stated, "one of my best friends used to work at NIH some years ago and he recommended me to his lab before he left. So, he left, and I came." We heard other comparable accounts.

The transnational nature of biomedical research is also reflected in what postdoctoral students plan to do once their training is completed. It is often assumed that many developing country NIH postdocs are eager to remain in the United States. Many do, but most do not. More interesting, if perhaps unremarkable, was that most interviewees were open to consider alternatives, whether in the United States, their own countries or, if the opportunity was right, in third countries. This is not altogether surprising since many young scientists received some or all of their doctoral education in countries other than their own or the United States, with some having attended universities or done postdoctoral work in several countries. For these young scientists, selecting a country in which to work was not very different from choosing in which country to do a postdoc. Among the factors influencing their decision-making are how much will they be compensated, how interesting will the work be, and what are the position's long-term career prospects. Family considerations are also involved; several interviewees suggested that families, in particular spouses, had a great deal of weight in the decision making process.

This being said, our interviews revealed a marked divide by country of origin (developing and developed) in intentions to stay or not in the United States. Scientists from the developing world, by and large, were far more likely to want to stay in America than those from advanced countries, whether in Europe (Germany, France), Asia (Japan, Korea), Israel or Australia. However, scientists from these latter countries, while exhibiting a strong return preference, were also open to other options. For example, an Australian biochemist was considering either returning home or seeking employment in the United Kingdom. Among developing country scientists from countries such as India and China who had received advanced U.S. degrees, the desire to stay was sharpest. Motivations are quite complex, however, and often reflect realistic evaluations of employment prospects at home, or even potential conflictive situations associated with individual role changes. A Yugoslavian female entomologist could not see herself returning home partly because of a deteriorated political and economic situation. More important, perhaps, was that she perceived she had become more independent by having lived by herself away from home. She could not face going back to live with an "overly protective family."

The decision to stay or return, or whether to work in a third country, is often also contingent on the type of work the scientist is seeking. A German zoologist was willing to consider all sorts of national destinations as long as they were in academia. This was true as well for a Chinese molecular biologist that decided not to return to China because he had received and accepted an offer to teach at a Canadian university. While expressing interest in staying in the United States, a

Russian biochemist was not beyond considering employment in Sweden where human genome scientists were being recruited with very attractive offers. A cell biologist from the United Kingdom, although making quite clear his desire to return, felt that he would have to consider whatever came up, in the United States or elsewhere. An extreme example is that of a Chinese scientist on a J–1 visa. While he believed that he could apply for and probably receive a U.S. permanent visa, he felt that "no one country can make me feel better than another, so I don't care if I can stay [in the United States] or if I have to go back to China."

The role of family on the stay or return decision is complex and appears to be rooted in the family life cycle and the capacity of family members to adapt to life in a foreign country, including language ability. A Korean bacteriologist was under pressure from his wife to return because she could not master the English language. In contrast, a Chinese molecular biologists felt compelled to stay in the United States because her son, who was born in the United States while she pursued her doctorate, would have been at great disadvantage in China due to his inability to speak or write Chinese. Other foreign potsdocs planned to remain in the United States because they had married American citizens.

That the motivations to stay are complex is made evident by a Swedish computational biologist who provided a more elaborate and subtle explanation as to why many foreign scientists, especially from developing countries, decide to stay in the United States. In her view, the reasons go beyond higher salaries or better research opportunities. They have much to do with the potential for social mobility foreign scientists find in the United States, as opposed to the more rigid social structures characterizing more traditional societies. As she stated:

People born in America take their freedom for granted. This is the freest country, other than the Netherlands, that I have ever experienced. And I have traveled quite a bit. Americans think foreigners stay in the United States because of the salary, but it is much more than that. For example, there was this Chinese postdoc I worked with when I was a postdoc at the university. He could barely speak. Some people treated him like he was an idiot and made him feel like he was at the bottom. But he was bright and he learned the language and he excelled and no one could make him go back to that submissive and inferior state of mind. People go through this and feel like a survivor. They have the freedom to improve themselves. It is not just salary or culturally drawn, it is self-esteem drawn. Most foreigners who come here would not go through the immigration hell unless they wanted to get their green card and stay in the United States.

Immigration Pathways and Legal Mechanisms

There are several ways in which foreign scientists can work at NIH for extended periods of time or remain permanently in the United States. An occasional foreign scientist may be offered a tenure-track position; others are sponsored by NIH directly for an H-1B temporary work visa. And additional status adjustment avenues are open for postdoctoral fellows and other exchange visitors. Immigration attorneys are particularly adept at guiding foreign applicants through the labyrinth of regulations. We went to the lawyers for insights into the process. One of these, recognized as one of the leading immigration attorneys in the Washington metropolitan area, told us that of his 1997 case load of some 500 cases, approximately 50 were NIH scientists.

The J-1 Visa

Immigration attorneys pointed out that the great majority of foreign scientists and trainees at NIH now come as Visiting Scientists, Associates, or Fellows under the sponsorship of NIH's Fogarty International Center on J-1 exchange visitor visas financed by [former] USIA. They noted that this visa has a number of advantages over other temporary, nonimmigrant visas, such as the H-1B (specialty worker) and L-1 (intercompany transferee). For example, unlike the other two visa types, a J-1 visa can be obtained without initial approval of a visa petition by the INS because the J-1 visa applicant's U.S. sponsor provides the required Certificate of Eligibility for Exchange Visitor Status. Also, the J-1 visa is free from the prevailing wage, posting, and record-keeping requirements of the H-1B. Further, employment authorization can be obtained for the J-1's dependents as J-2s, which is not possible for the spouse or children of an H-1B or an L-1 visa holder.

On the other hand, lawyers explained, the J-1 visa poses difficulties for NIH foreign exchange visitors who decide that they wish to extend their stay in this country beyond the expiration of their visas. Because the primary objective of the exchange visitor program is to assist the development of friendly, cooperative ties between the United States and other nations, the U.S. government takes the official position that this objective can be met only if exchange visitors return to their home countries to apply and share the knowledge and skills they have acquired in the United States. Therefore, foreigners who have participated in an exchange visitor program financed by an agency of the United States Government are required to return home for two years before they are eligible to obtain either an H–1B or an L–1 nonimmigrant visa or permanent resident status in the United States.

However, there are various ways to obtain a waiver of this requirement. The one especially favored by immigration lawyers dealing with clients at NIH is to have "an interested U.S. government agency"— that is, NIH—ask the U.S. State Department (formerly USIA) to recommend a waiver to INS on the grounds that the exchange visitor's continued presence and work in the United States are important to the national interest.

A number of attorneys remarked that NIH used to be very reluctant to do this because it was felt that for foreign scientists to remain in the United States and not return home would cause a "brain drain" for their home countries. However, these lawyers explained, NIH officials concluded about ten years ago that in many cases there was insufficient scientific infrastructure in scientists' home countries—especially those in the third world—to adequately support the scientists' research and to effectively apply any resulting products, and that therefore it would be at best pointless and at worst wasteful to insist that all foreign scientists go home right away at the expiration of their visas. This led to a shift in NIH policy that has greatly facilitated the process of obtaining waivers for foreign scientists. NIH's decision to be more liberal regarding the recommendation that waivers be issued so that foreign trainees could adjust their visa status was confirmed to us during an interview on the record with Dr. Michael Gottesman, NIH's Deputy Director for Intramural Affairs.

For the J–1 visa waiver to be processed, the relevant U.S. government agency must receive a formal non-objection letter issued through diplomatic channels from the country of nationality or last permanent residence of the foreign scientist, as well as a recommendation of a waiver provided by NIH. For NIH to send the latter, the applicant must have been accepted into a residency program (in the case of a physician) or have received a job offer from an entity other than NIH.

Applicants generally must return to their home countries for 3 to 6 months while waiting for the approval process to be completed before returning to the United States.

The O-1 Temporary Visa Route

Another viable option used by attorneys for NIH clients wishing to change visa status is the O-1 temporary work visa, which is available to persons who have "extraordinary ability in the sciences, arts, education, business, or athletics which has been demonstrated by sustained national or international acclaim." If a J-1 holder is granted an O-1 visa, a waiver of the two-year return to home country requirement will not be necessary because this rule applies only to the granting of H or L visas and permanent resident status.

Attorneys commented that it is easier to assist clients associated with NIH than those connected with other biomedical institutions because the NIH affiliation greatly strengthens the argument that the foreign scientists will be working in the national interest and because at the time of petition the scientists are part of an entity that is in fact a recognized national interest. Further, these lawyers asserted that the credentials of NIH's foreign scientists are typically so impressive that few difficulties are encountered in helping them to change temporary visa category or to obtain permanent resident status.

The Contract Work Route

There is another category of foreign workers that relies on NIH as a transit route to the U.S. labor market. These are temporary foreign workers employed by NIH through its numerous contractors. These contract workers, often in the United States with H–1B visas for periods of up to six years—and said to number in the hundreds—often work side-by-side with permanent NIH staff providing support and development functions. It is reasonable to assume that this is also a permanent skilled immigration channel in that many of these contract workers are eventually sponsored for permanent U.S. residency by their American employers or otherwise manage to adjust their residency status through some other mechanism.

How many of these foreign contract workers are in fact biomedical scientists cannot be ascertained given the fragmented or nonexistent nature of the employment information and the fact that they are employed by private sector firms rather than by NIH directly. Our educated guess, however, is that many of these foreign workers could occupationally be classified as information technology specialists hired in part to cope with the exploding demands generated at NIH by the information revolution, on the one hand, and, with the more narrow requirements, on the other, of computational biology. As noted earlier, many of the so-called computational biologists working at NIH, some as postdoctoral fellows, have physical sciences and mathematics backgrounds and were often trained in Eastern Europe and the former Soviet Union.

Adjustment Strategies and Recent Trends

Lawyers described the strategies employed by NIH foreign scientists to extend their stays in the United States. Like their other clients, those from NIH often find their way to immigration attorneys through ethnic and country-of-origin networks that provide information and assistance. In this regard, one attorney said that at NIH "the Chinese Scholars Association is very effective, perhaps more so than we are." NIH foreign scientists also have linkages based on commonality of discipline, nature of research, and laboratory workplace. These scientists were described by attorneys as resourceful and adept at utilizing word of mouth and internet sources of information to locate potential jobs and legal assistance.

According to lawyers, some of the immigrant clients enter medical school residency programs with associated research, and some go to work in biotechnology firms. The majority, however, prefer to take research positions in academia if possible.

It was noted that it seems that for the past decade there have been more R&D biotech company staff working under contract at NIH on teams with American and foreign scientists with J-1 visas. In this way, biotech firms come to know and recruit U.S. and foreign workers who are using new research techniques. Universities also recruit, but less actively. Attorneys remarked that NIH very seldom sponsors foreign postdoctoral fellows for permanent residence based on positions offered them at NIH, and they felt that NIH should do this much more often in order to keep the expertise that these scientists possess.

Two recent trends were identified that involve immigration clients at NIH. In 1995, the People's Republic of China stopped agreeing to waive the requirement for Chinese NIH visiting fellows to return home because evidently none were doing so willingly. Also, a growing number of scientists from Russia, other former Soviet republics, and other Eastern European countries have been seeking to obtain U.S. permanent residence and citizenship.

Immigration attorneys generally regarded foreign scientists as a tremendous asset to NIH and the United States, describing them in such glowing terms as "incredibly impressive," "world leaders," and "topnotch." One characterized them as NIH's "backbone of research." Another declared that "having foreign scientists at NIH greatly enhances the global competitiveness of this country."

These lawyers did not think that the presence of foreign scientists in this country has a negative impact on the employment opportunities of American scientists. In fact, one even asserted the opposite:

> People of this caliber do not take existing jobs away from Americans; they only create more jobs for Americans by finding new paths and expanding areas of research.

None of the attorneys spoke of having difficulty with U.S. immigration policy. They commented that it is "fairly decent," works "expeditiously," and "meets the needs of the scientific community."

In contrast, they all expressed dissatisfaction with U.S. labor policy. One recommended that for prevailing wage purposes, a distinction needs to be made between the categories of profit and non-profit organizations, and that a special (non-profit) designation should be made for academic entities. Another felt that the Department of Labor (DOL) should not be dealing with professionals at such a specialized high level as biomedical scientists, and she noted that DOL procedural mechanisms "are all backed up, anyway."

Summary

Although very few foreign postdoctoral fellows manage to stay at NIH as permanent staff, many NIH former foreign postdoctoral trainees do remain in the United States by finding employment sponsors willing to assist them in overcoming the foreign residency condition associated with the J-1 visa.

- This process has been eased over the last ten years by a shift in NIH's policy that has entailed a greater willingness to recommend to the U.S. Department of State that foreign residency requirements for foreign fellows wishing to remain in the United States be waived.
- The process has been facilitated as well by the availability of the O–1 visa established by Congress in the Immigration Act of 1990.

Another route to permanent residency is indirectly provided by NIH to foreign scientists through private sector contractors.

- An unspecified number of foreign temporary highly skilled workers employed by NIH private-sector contractors also manage to adjust status to permanent residence.

6

Conclusions

The views presented by the range of persons interviewed during the course of this study provided perspectives useful for understanding the reasons for and the implications arising from the presence of foreign biomedical scientists, primarily as postdoctoral trainees, at NIH. These perceptions are also relevant to broader labor market issues associated with the employment prospects and working conditions of American biomedical scientists, as well as for U.S. immigration and labor policies.

Given the nature of the study's qualitative approach, the validity of the conclusions that can be drawn is largely predicated on the degree to which the various categories of interviewees concurred in their perceptions or interpretations of experiences. It should also be noted that certain key informants were privy to, or, in fact, had made management decisions or implemented policies to which others were oblivious. Good examples were the NIH senior administration officials with institutional memories who were responsible for and had observed the effects of management and policy decisions. Junior postdoctoral fellows had nothing to say regarding such matters.

The strength of our research design lay in its ability to shed light on a discrete set of issues by systematically drawing on the collective interpretations of events and processes of various categories of individuals looking at the same situation from different perspectives. These perspectives, together with a general appreciation of the overall institutional environment of NIH, mostly drawn from a review of the literature, selected statistical data, and ethnographic participant observations, allowed us to configure a nuanced interpretation that goes well beyond what could be reasonably expected from anecdotal information.

Several universally held perceptions emerged from our interviews. The first was that NIH offers training opportunities to postdoctoral and other foreign scientists primarily in compliance with its mandate to advance biomedical knowledge and to forge international research linkages. The work of NIH in these respects was without exception viewed as admirable and well performed. The second area in which there was consensus was that the foreign biomedical scientists that come to the United States, whether as postdoctoral fellows at NIH or elsewhere, or as students in American universities, are in the main quite talented and extremely hardworking. There was a range of opinion regarding skill levels by nationality, but foreign biomedical scientists, notably from Europe and some East Asia countries such as Japan, were regarded as particularly well trained. Some individuals questioned the academic training adequacy and general skill level of biomedical scientists from some countries (China and India, for example), but were consistent in their assessment that regardless of initial differences, foreign scientists by and large tend to catch up quickly with their American counterparts.

Another nearly unanimous conclusion that can derived from the information offered by persons with first-hand NIH experience was that compensation and working conditions for foreign and American postdoctoral fellows do not differ in any appreciable way. The various stipend levels can be found in the NIH webpage and other readily accessible sources of information, and they vary only as a function of years of experience. Some minor differences in compensation may be related to funding sources: that is, if trainees receive stipends from their governments or employers, rather than from NIH, they may be paid more or less what others get. Net compensation may also be affected by international tax treaties that preclude the Internal Revenue Service from taxing a foreigner's income while in the United States, or by differential tax rates applied by foreign countries to the stipends of their nationals while at NIH.

Another common conclusion was that working conditions for foreign and American postdocs are essentially the same. The only differences of note arose from variations in type of research conducted according to laboratory (e.g., animals may be used in some and not in others), as well as from specific assignments within laboratories. The latter are often dictated by research needs and laboratory chiefs' management styles. One exception noted by many informants is that American postdocs are usually selected over foreign postdocs for written and presentation assignments because of their superior command of English and greater self-assurance in U.S. forums.

Foreign biomedical postdocs did not seem to differ from their American counterparts in any marked way in terms of disciplines and specialty areas. Both seemed to be drawn from the full kaleidoscope of biomedical research areas, except that there appeared to be a disproportionate representation of foreigners in the emerging field of computational biology. Many computational biologists were said to be drawn from the former Soviet Union and other ex-communist Eastern European countries where training in the physical sciences, as well as in mathematics, was purported to be more rigorous than in the United States and other source countries of foreign scientists. It might well be that the primary training of at least some of these scientists was in fields other than biology. In some NIH institutes and centers, such as the National Library of Medicine, we were able to ascertain that foreign information technology scientists hold many of the contract research and support positions.

A number of individuals—mainly, but not solely foreign scientists—suggested that NIH offers postdoctoral fellowships in part because they provide a relatively cheap source of highly skilled labor. According to this view, were it not for the foreign scientists, biomedical research costs at NIH (as well as in other American research laboratories) would be considerably higher. The argument is that because of the availability of foreign postdocs, American postdoctoral scientists are prevented from commanding considerably higher stipends solely as a function of supply and demand forces. A complementary argument as to why foreign postdocs are sought was based on the perceptions that foreign scientists are very hard working and likely to work longer hours than American scientists.

However, we feel confident in concluding that the main thrust behind the foreign training program is NIH's desire to comply with its institutional mission of advancing biomedical knowledge and creating international biomedical research linkages. There was no evidence, other than conjectural interpretations primarily advanced by some foreign scientists, that NIH offers postdoctoral fellowship to foreign scientists to undercut employment opportunities or working conditions for American scientists; nor was there any factual basis for believing that foreign postdoctoral scientists work at NIH under less satisfactory conditions or are compensated any less (at the same level of seniority) than U.S. scientists.

This is not to say, however, that the presence of foreign scientists at NIH, and in American research laboratories more generally, does not affect the employment and working conditions of American scientists. Many of the persons interviewed were cognizant of a far more complex and elusive picture when the issue is placed within a broader labor market context. As noted earlier, many alluded to the negative impact the presence of foreign scientists has on the implicit or overt ability of American biomedical scientists, at NIH and elsewhere, to bargain for higher salaries and stipends. This situation is not likely to improve in the future: as educational systems worldwide continue to improve and graduate more and more well-trained scientists, the potential supply of skilled foreign biomedical scientists seeking to come to and stay in the United States will rise. To achieve their long-term objective of remaining in the United States (where salaries and working conditions are better than in many of their home countries, particularly in the developing world), foreign scientists are more than willing to work a grueling number of hours each day. They are also willing to accept modest stipends that are, in many cases, much higher than what they would have earned as well-established professionals in their countries.

While acknowledging that the situation described above may hold true in the short run, most of the interviewees would contend that it could lead to spurious and erroneous conclusions concerning the long-term picture. The exact opposite conclusion can be reached when due consideration is given to the beneficial impact that the presence of foreign scientists has on the development of U.S. biomedical science and biotechnology industry. The vast majority of persons interviewed, whether foreign or American, were convinced that in a more dynamic scenario a constant influx of foreign scientists, particularly if they stay in the United States, could only result in enhanced American international competitiveness in biomedicine and biotechnology. This development, in turn, would considerably expand employment opportunities and improve compensation levels and working conditions for American scientists by increasing the size of the economic pie.

This is even more so if the United States can without delay fill scientific research openings in emerging and highly specialized fields, such as computational biology, by recruiting foreign scientists with the requisite skills, and thus maintain its international competitive advantage. According to this reasoning, although individual American biomedical scientists might be hurt by labor market competition from foreign scientists, as a whole the American biomedical and biotechnology research community gains, as does the U.S. economy. A number of interviewees alluded to the benefits that accrue to the U.S. economy from the entrepreneurial spirit of foreign scientists and to the commercial advantages they vest in American firms operating abroad because of their better understanding of foreign cultures and markets.

A concern of some was that under certain circumstances the United States economy might suffer from the presence of foreign biomedical scientists in American laboratories. There was some trepidation that when these scientists return home, they might take with them know-how developed here that could be used to strengthen the scientific prowess of overseas competitors. Ghosts of past opportunities missed—to Japan in the electronic industry, for example—were obviously at play. While this concern has been voiced before, those that addressed this issue in the course of the study were only mildly concerned. They tended to conclude, as a general rule, that the fear of scientific and technological loss is exaggerated and that, regardless of the seepage, the United States gains far more from the contributions made by foreign scientists than what it loses via those who do not come here to stay.

Many individuals also mentioned the unwillingness of promising young American students to pursue research careers in the demanding biomedical research field as one of the primary reasons why foreign scientists are in such demand in the U.S. labor force. This trend was attributed to several causes, but mainly to the desire of American students to enter into more financially rewarding and less arduous professions, such as law and business. This situation, which was said by some to be leading into a vicious circle, is in part explained by the opportunity structure of the U.S. economy and how it distributes its financial and prestige rewards. As fewer American students select biomedical careers, U.S. training institutions are forced to increasingly rely on the admission of foreign students to maintain enrollment levels (and hence, ensure the survival of graduate academic departments) and satisfy labor market demand. And as the number of foreign scientists in U.S. universities and laboratories rise, the circle is completed as the number of Americans continues to decline, as has happened in engineering schools across the United States.

The preceding view is essentially premised on the assumption that there is a dearth of U.S. biomedical scientists (an interpretation supported by currently low unemployment rates in these fields). An alternate line of thought among some was that the United States could potentially achieve a reasonable balance between the supply of and demand for U.S. biomedical scientists. A troublesome downside to the trend of so many foreign biomedical scientists working in the United States is that American educational institutions and industry can continue to avoid coming to terms with the need to bring into balance the U.S. demand for and supply of biomedical research education. Some put the blame squarely on a bloated U.S. higher education system that produces more scientists in too many graduate programs than the economy can efficiently absorb.

One solution would be to contain the growth of biomedical education, perhaps by reducing admissions or closing graduate schools. One precedent is what has happened with the closing of many of the nation's dental schools. This view tacitly assumes, of course, that the U.S. economy currently has an excess number of biomedical scientists and that foreign scientists contribute to the existence of an even bigger surplus. It could be argued that where it not for the abundant supply of foreign scientists, industry might be forced to offer more rewarding career opportunities to entice more Americans to pursue biomedical research careers.

Some of the more obvious symptoms of this problem are the lengthy periods that students currently spend, first, in graduate education, and, after graduation, in postdoctoral training. Both are indicative of substantial underemployment in the biomedical doctoral ranks. In fact, a few persons indicated that there are signs of the emergence of a biomedical postdoctoral research underclass. This underclass, heavily but not exclusively populated by foreign scientists, is concentrated in lesser-ranked universities that manage to keep their research laboratories operating by offering postdoctoral appointments to the least promising scientists that, barring other options, migrate from one underrated laboratory to the next. The end goal of many of the foreign postdocs in the training circuit is to adjust their immigrant status and remain in the United States.

This study can only offer some modest contributions to the raging controversy as to whether the United States is producing too many biomedical doctorates, or whether the influx of foreign scientists is making the situation worse. Several careful statistical studies, including the one conducted by the Committee on Dimensions, Causes, and Implications of Recent Trends in the Careers of Life Scientists of the National Research Council, suggest that this might be the case. One caveat is that, as in the information technology field, the economic cycle, as noted by several individuals, may have a significant bearing on the demand for biomedical scientific research talent. So also, it might be noted, does the dollar amount of the level of appropriations made by Congress in support of biomedical research, given the key role of the federal government as its patron.

In addition to the above, this study has detected three especially interesting institutional patterns of some significance for U.S. immigration and labor policies. These are that:

- The growth since the early 1980s in the number of foreign, as well as American, biomedical postdoctoral trainees at NIH was part of NIH's strategy to cope with federally mandated limits in the size of the government employment work force that was imposed in spite of sizable NIH budget increases;
- NIH's foreign postdoctoral training program is a de facto seamless and efficient recruitment mechanism whereby American academe and industry can, at minimal cost, indirectly evaluate, select and hire biomedical scientists from a large and constantly renewing pool of foreign candidates that includes talented and promising young biomedical scientists from around the world; and
- NIH's foreign postdoctoral training program serves to attain selected public policy objectives as formalized in several recent federal legislative actions. These include the Patent and Trademark Laws Amendments of 1980 (Public Law 96–517, also known as the Bayh-Dole Act), the Federal Technology Transfer Act of 1986, and the Immigration Reform Act of 1990.

Manpower Strategy

Since the 1980s, NIH has been facing a dilemma: while in constant dollars its budget has being increasing at a faster rate than that of most other federal agencies (except perhaps the defense budget during President Reagan's first term), it has had to contend with federally mandated reductions in force. This has meant that to sustain programmatic growth, NIH has had no choice but to contract out many of its support and research functions. This personnel strategy was consistent with the Reagan's administration policy objective of privatizing as many government functions as possible, while managing to indirectly increase personnel to carry out an expanded workload.

As many interviewees suggested, the growth in the number of foreign postdocs since the early 1980s appears to have been a complement to NIH's personnel strategy. As trainees, foreign postdocs did not press against staffing ceilings and, therefore, they have granted NIH a measure of personnel hiring flexibility.

It is also tempting to conclude that the appearance and rapid growth in the number of American postdoctoral trainees at NIH under the IRTA program may have also been part of an ongoing institutional strategy to accommodate rising personnel requirements. This resulted from increased funding at the same time as pressures to contain the growth of the federal work force continued unabated. The policy to reduce the size of the federal work force, while initiated during the Reagan years, was also embraced by the administrations of Presidents George H. W. Bush and William J. Clinton. It does not seem entirely coincidental that NIH was granted authority to train U.S. postdocs in 1986. This was the time when the rate of growth of foreign postdoctoral trainees was most dramatic, increasing by 65 percent between 1980 and 1986. The first IRTA American postdoctoral trainees arrived at the Bethesda campus in 1990.

Recruitment Mechanism

Although it was not originally designed with this purpose in mind, NIH's foreign postdoctoral training program serves as an ideal recruitment funnel for potential U.S. employers in academe and industry. NIH receives thousands of applications each year from young scientists in countries the world over to fill some 2,000 training slots. NIH laboratory chiefs and principal investigators make a first cut and select the most promising candidates according to their evaluations of applicant's credentials (including academic background, institutions where they were trained, recommendations of foreign colleagues, etc.), who are then invited to come to Bethesda. They also select trainees from among foreign graduates of American universities. In fact, foreign graduates of American educational institutions comprise a large minority of Visiting Fellows at NIH.

Foreign trainee professional performance and promise is monitored and evaluated by NIH laboratory chiefs, as well as by outsiders in the broader biomedical research community (as judged by publication record, presentations at professional meetings, and peer reviews). Furthermore, close professional ties link laboratory chiefs with potential American employers. The latter are always on the lookout for promising young scientists. Through their contacts with laboratory chiefs, employers can verify the scientific promise of potential employees, whose skills have been closely evaluated by trusted professional peers in a U.S. research setting. Laboratory chiefs may also take the initiative and recommend particularly strong candidates to colleagues in academe or industry working in related fields. Thus, NIH acts as a unique federal testing ground for American employers who are thus enabled to select from among promising foreign scientists already familiar with the latest American laboratory scientific procedures and work routines. All that employers need to do is process the needed paper work to secure temporary or permanent work visas for their future foreign-origin employees.

Vehicle for the Attainment of Public Policy Objectives

It can be argued that NIH's decision to begin relaxing its former policy of not granting waivers to the two-year foreign residency requirement associated with the issuance of J–1 visas was done partly in response to one of the policy objectives of the Immigration Reform Act of 1990. The policy objective in question was to increase the number of temporary and permanent skilled immigrants through employment-based criteria, including the permanent immigration preferences, where the number of admissions has been substantial.

Between 1991 and 1997, for example, permanent admissions under the first employment preference (including "Aliens with extraordinary ability" and "Outstanding professors and researchers") increased from 580 to 3,814 primary beneficiaries (excluding family members), or by more than 500 percent in a five-year period (Kramer 1999:7). Likewise, the number of nonimmigrant admissions for skilled foreign workers, including "Workers with extraordinary ability" (O–1 visa) and

"Specialty occupations: Professionals" (H–1B visas) rose appreciably between 1994 and 1996. Among the former, the number of admissions increased from 5,029 in 1996, to 7,177 in 1998, or by 43 percent, whereas among the latter, they jumped from 105,899 to 144,458, or by 36 percent (Kramer 1999:29). These are the employment-based permanent and temporary immigration categories under which foreign biomedical research scientists are most likely to adjust their temporary immigration status.

The relaxation of the two-year foreign residency requirement on the part of NIH was also consistent with the policy objectives embodied in the Bayh-Dole Act and the Federal Technology Transfer Act. The purpose of these legislative measures was to allow American universities and industry to commercially benefit from government-sponsored research. By the late 1990s, NIH's Office of Technology Transfer had negotiated numerous CRADAs (cooperative research and development agreements) with industry to facilitate the transfer of technologies developed in its Bethesda laboratories. It is reasonable to assume that some former NIH postdoctoral trainees, both American and foreign, may have been instrumental in the establishment of cooperative ventures: They were familiar with, and probably participated in, the development of the biomedical technologies being shared under the CRADAs. Their presence in private sector laboratories facilitates the sharing of technological skills and ensures institutional collaboration by easing ongoing working relationship between the former postdocs and their NIH mentors, as well as with their new employers in industry.

Thus, by adjusting their immigration status, some former foreign postdoctoral trainees help the United States achieve two distinct but related public policy objectives. One is to increase the number of highly skilled foreign immigrants, as called for in the Immigration Reform Act of 1990. Secondly, by moving from NIH laboratories to biotechnology laboratories, particularly those associated with the pharmaceutical industry, former foreign postdoctoral trainees also contribute to the goal of enhancing U.S. international competitiveness. The end result is the creation of more jobs and wealth in the American economy.

Appendix A

Foreign Scientist Training Opportunities at NIH

Summary of Categories and Conditions

NIH Visiting Program (for foreign scientists): Provides opportunities for biomedical researchers at all levels of their careers to participate in the varied research activities of NIH. Through this program, scientists are invited to NIH to conduct collaborative research in their medical specialties. The Visiting Program is the largest and most longstanding of NIH's international research and training programs. Each year, more than 2,000 scientists from foreign countries conduct collaborative research at NIH. Candidates are invited to participate by senior NIH scientists, based on the research needs of the host laboratory. There are three categories of Visiting Program participants. In addition, the NIH accepts **Guest Researchers** and **Special Volunteers**, who have other sources of support for their research or training at NIH. The three categories of Visiting Program participants are:

Visiting Fellows—scientists with doctoral degrees or their equivalents and three years or less of relevant experience;

Visiting Associates—scientist with three years to six years of postdoctoral research experience;

Visiting Scientists—scientists with six or more years of postdoctoral research experience.

While Visiting Fellows are usually appointed for two years (with the potential for extension for up to 5 years), one-year awards may be considered. The fellowship period is renewable for up to five years. Renewals are based on merit and are subject to approval by the sponsor and Institute Director. All renewals are contingent upon visa limitations and compliance with U.S. immigration regulations. U.S. citizens are not eligible for the Visiting Fellow award.[1] Visiting Associates and Visiting Scientists appointments are generally for an initial two-year period but may be made for a shorter period. Appointments may be renewed; however, the total length of an appointment normally may not exceed five years. Extension of appointment for 90 days or less may be requested provided sponsor has strong justification. There is an overall limitation of eight years that an individual may remain at NIH without being designated as tenure-track or permanent/tenure status. This includes time spent in all categories of awards or appointments at NIH. All renewals are subject to applicable visa restrictions. All participants must be proficient in the use and understanding of both written and spoken English. An award or appointment to the Visiting Program must be requested by a senior scientist in one of NIH's intramural laboratories. The senior scientist serves as the participant's sponsor during the period of award or appointment. Stipends or salary schedules are based on levels of experience.

Individuals interested in the Visiting Program should write to NIH senior scientists working in their area of expertise, enclosing a resume and brief description of background and research interests. Information on research being conducted by NIH scientists may be obtained from the *NIH Scientific Directory and Annual Bibliography.*

Stipends or salary schedules are based on levels of experience. The present range is:

Visiting Fellows:
$25,000 to $30,000 for less than one year of postdoctoral experience.
$26,500 to $32,000 for 1 to 2 years of postdoctoral experience.
$28,000 to $34,000 for 2 to 3 years of postdoctoral experience.
$29,000 to $36,000 for 3 to 4 years of postdoctoral experience.
$31,000 to $38,000 for 4 to 5 years of postdoctoral experience.

For each year the fellowship is continued, the stipend may be increased by $1,500. Increases above this amount must be approved by the Institute Scientific Director.

While Visiting Fellows receive a stipend, they are considered non-employees. Visiting Associates and Visiting Scientists receive a salary, and are considered employees of the NIH, receive a salary and, depending on the length of appointment, receive most of the benefits available to employees of the U.S. government. The latter two engage in collaborative research.

Salaries for Visiting Associates and Scientists are based on each candidate's qualifications. Stipends will be paid for professional scientific duties similar to those performed by professional Institute staff members in the Civil Service assigned to health research and investigation. Visiting Associate stipends are rounded from the nearest thousand dollars and range from GS–9, Step 1 to GS–12, Step 10. Visiting Scientist stipends should range from the GS–12, Step 1 level to the maximum allowable salary of the General Schedule.

At each anniversary date, both Visiting Associates and Visiting Scientists are eligible for a stipend increase of $1,000 for meeting research goals and $1,500 for significantly exceeding research goals. Increases in excess of $1,500 require extensive justification (Approval level per delegation). Visiting Associates and Visiting Scientists receive the comparability increase at the same level as GS employees. They do not receive locality pay.

In some institutes (e.g., NINDS) predoctoral Visiting Fellowships are available for non-U.S. citizens enrolled in accredited U.S. universities. Supplemental stipend awards are available to qualified predoctoral and doctoral candidates that will supplement a non-NIH awarded fellowship. Total stipends may not exceed the authorized stipend for NIH awarded predoctoral or doctoral Visiting Fellows with similar years education or postdoctoral experience.

Guest Researcher Position: The purpose is to make research and study facilities of the Institute readily available to the local, national, and international scientific community, especially qualified academic scientists and engineers. Guest Researchers use facilities to further their own research or training by using equipment and resources which are otherwise not available to them. They do not provide a service for the institute.

Eligibility: Guest Researchers must be qualified technically trained academic scientists, engineers, students or other scientifically trained specialists. Guest Researchers are usually sponsored and paid by an outside organization. They may, however, be self-supporting scientists not being sponsored by an outside organization provided the appropriate Lab/Branch Chief certifies their research credentials are appropriate, they have adequate financial resources, and the research will be of direct benefit to the Guest Researcher and not for the specific purpose of performing services for NIEHS. Guest Researchers may be non-U.S. citizens. Minimum education for non-U.S. citizen is a Masters Degree or equivalent.

> **Compensation**: Guest Researchers are not paid by the Government since they do not perform any services for the Government.

> **Appointment Length**: Guest Researchers assignments are usually for 1 or 2 years but may be extended upon approval.

> **Approval Authority:** Division Director

> **Other**: Note: It is never appropriate or legal for a Guest Researcher to be on a B–2 (tourist) visa.

Special Volunteer: To provide a mechanism whereby individuals can volunteer their services to the NIEHS but receive no direct compensation from NIH/NIEHS. Special Volunteers may, however, receive support from outside sources *with approval.*

> **Eligibility**: Anyone over 16 years old but under 18 years old must have a valid work permit. Nepotism policies apply. Special Volunteers may be anyone volunteering for research, clerical assignments, technical assistance or any other activities necessary to carry out the authorized functions of NIEHS. Special Volunteers over 16 years old but under 18 years old must have a valid work permit. Special Volunteers may be a non-U.S. citizen. Minimum education requirement for non-U.S. citizen is a Masters Degree or equivalent.

> **Appointment Length**: Special Volunteer assignments are usually for 1 or 2 years but may be extended upon approval.

> **Approval Authority**: Division Director.

> **Other:** Note: It is never appropriate or legal for a Special Volunteer to be on a B–2 (tourist) visa.

Scholars in Residence Program: Each year the Fogarty International Center invites six to ten eminent scientists to the NIH to interact with the scientific community and to conduct studies of importance to biomedicine and international health. In March 1997-February 1998 there were 13 Scholars in Residence serving for staggered periods of time. Four were from Israel, two each from Japan and Germany, and one each from the United Kingdom and Canada. Three were Americans or were associated with U.S. institutions.

Exchange Scientists: One of these programs is the National Cancer Institute Scientist Exchange Program which promotes research collaboration between established American and foreign scientists. It supports exchange visits of U.S. cancer researchers to foreign laboratories or foreign cancer researchers to U.S. laboratories for periods of one week to six months.

Visas

Visiting Program participants who are foreign nationals must have a visa that permits training or employment in the United States. Most foreign nationals in the program have one of the following nonimmigrant visas: J–1 (Exchange Visitor), F–1 (student – for practical training after award of doctoral degree), H1-B (nonimmigrant worker in a specialty occupation), and O–1 (extraordinary ability in the sciences). Visiting Fellows are ineligible for H1-B or O–1 visas.

Under the NIH's Exchange Visitor Program (J–1 visa – Research Scholar category), any clinical responsibilities are limited to incidental patient contact, and credit for medical specialty board certification is not available. To have full patient contact, and credit for medical specialty board certification, foreign scientists at NIH must conduct their research under a J–1 visa sponsored by the Educational Commission for Foreign Medical Graduates (ECFMG) in those programs at NIH that meet graduate medical education or training accreditation standards.

Taxes

All Visiting Program participants must pay U.S. income taxes, unless they are exempted by an income tax treaty between the United

States and their country of citizenship or legal legal permanent residence. Although the tax assessment differs according to stipend/salary level (higher levels are taxed at higher rates), Visiting Program participants can expect to pay at least 20 percent of their stipend/salary in federal income tax. All participants, including those exempted from federal tax, must pay state income taxes, depending on their state of residence. Individuals holding an H–1B or O–1 visa also must pay Social Security tax.

Vacation and Sick Leave

Visiting Fellows may be granted excuse absence at the discretion of their sponsors, except during the final two weeks of the award period. In addition to federal holidays, Visiting Associates and Visiting Scientists receive 13 working days of annual (holiday) leave and 13 working days of sick leave each year.

Health Insurance

All Visiting Program participants must have some form of health insurance; J–1 visa holders (and accompanying dependents) are required by regulation to be covered by health insurance, including medical evacuation and repatriation of remains. The NIH pays for basic coverage for Visiting Fellows and dependents who accompany them.

Visiting Associates and Visiting Scientists may join one of the health plans available at the NIH under the Federal Government's health benefit plans if their initial appointment is for longer than 12 months. They pay part of the cost, although the actual amount will depend on the plan selected. Visiting Associates and Visiting Scientists on a J–1 visa must purchase a separate policy for medical evacuation and repatriation of remains. Those on an initial appointment of 12 months or less are responsible for making their own health insurance arrangements and paying the full cost involved.

Source: Verbatim transcript of information provided on NIH's webpage.

Appendix B

Fogarty International Center (FIC) Programs

Program	Summary	Eligibility	Scope of Support
FIC AIDS International Training and Research Program (AITRP)	Enables U.S. universities and other research institutions to provide HIV/AIDS-related training to scientists and health professionals from developing nations and to forge collaborative ties with research institutions in countries highly affected by the AIDS virus.	Applicants must be principal investigators of an NIH-sponsored AIDS or AIDS-related research project grant or project directors of an NIH center grant or cooperative agreement that will be active during the grant award period.	Awards provided for: (1) training in epidemiological concepts, methods, field studies, and research related to AIDS that will lead to the M.S. or Ph.D. degree; (2) short-term comprehensive courses in epidemiology for health professionals with an emphasis on AIDS; (3) training in laboratory procedures and research techniques related to AIDS for individuals with the M.S. or Ph.D. degree; and (4) practical and applied short-term training related to AIDS conducted in the foreign country for professionals, technicians and allied-health professionals.
International Training and Research Program in Environmental and Occupational Health	In collaboration with the National Institute of Environmental Health Sciences and the National Institute for Occupational Safety and Health, Centers for Disease Control and Prevention, the FIC funds nonprofit public or private institutions to support international training and	U.S. nonprofit private or public academic institutions; and other nonprofit institutions that satisfy the academic requirements of the program.	Institutional awards are provided at a funding level not to exceed $150,000 per year in direct and indirect costs for the first year, for a maximum of 5 years. Awards support: (1) predoctoral research training related to environmental and occupation health that will lead to the M.S. or Ph.D. degree (at a U.S. institution);

Program	Summary	Eligibility	Scope of Support
	research programs in general environmental health and occupational health for foreign health scientists, clinicians, epidemiologists, toxicologists, engineers, industrial hygienists, chemists and allied-health workers. The program complements ongoing environmental and occupational health research and training efforts of the NIH and other agencies of the U.S. Government.		(2) postdoctoral research training in procedures, research projects, andtechniques related to environmental and occupational disease and injury (at a U.S. institution or in the trainees home country); (3) participation in advanced research training conducted by U.S. faculty in the host country and short-term, in-country training at the host U.S. institution.
International Training and Research Program in Population and Health	In cooperation with the National Institute of Child Health and Human Development (NICHD), the FIC funds U.S. nonprofit public or private institutions to support international training and research in population-related sciences. The program enables NIH grant recipients to extend the geographic base of research and training efforts to developing nations, in support of international population priorities.	Applicants must be a principal investigator of an NIH-sponsored research project grant, project director of an NIH center grant, program project grant or cooperative agreement that will be active during the proposed award period. In some cases, applications from recipients of research contracts related to population that will be funded during at least 1 year of the proposed award period will be considered.	Institutional awards are provided at a funding level not to exceed $150,000 per year in direct costs for the first year, for a maximum of 5 years. Awards support: (1) pre-doctoral training in research related to populations (at a U.S. institution); (2) postdoctoral training in laboratory procedures and techniques related to population research (at a U.S. institution or in the trainees home country); and (3) participation in advanced research training conducted by U.S. faculty in the host

Program	Summary	Eligibility	Scope of Support
			country and short-term, in-country training at the host U.S. Institution.
Minority International Research Training (MIRT) Grant	In cooperation with the NIH Office of Research on Minority Health, the FIC funds a MIRT Program to provide opportunities for international research and training for minorities underrepresented in the scientific professions. Institutional training grants are provided to U.S. colleges and universities to support undergraduate and graduate training at foreign institutions. Awards are also provided to faculty members to conduct independent research abroad and to serve as mentors to students abroad.	Two- or four-year domestic colleges or universities may apply individually or as a consortium. Student and faculty participants must be U.S. citizens or permanent residents and minorities that are underrepresented in the biomedical research professions (i.e., African and Hispanic Americans, Native Americans, Alaskan Natives and Pacific Islanders). They may include under graduate students pursuing life science curricula; students pursuing doctoral degrees in biomedical or behavioral sciences; and faculty members in the biomedical and behavioral sciences.	Awards to support research and training at foreign institutions range from 8 to 12 weeks for undergraduates and 3 to 12 months for pre-doctoral students, postdoctoral scientists and more established faculty. Each of the training grants will not exceed a total of $400,000 per year, including direct and indirect costs.
International Research Fellowship	The International Research Fellowship Program provides opportunities for postdoctoral scientists from emerging democracies, who are in the formative stages of their research career to extend their	Candidates are proposed by national or regional nominating committees established in Africa, Asia, (except China, South Korea, India, and Japan), Latin America, the Middle East (except Israel	Awards are for 12 months, renewable for an additional 12 months with the approval of the sponsor. Stipends range from $22,000 to $32,000 per year, based on the level of previous re-

Program	Summary	Eligibility	Scope of Support
	research experience in a U.S. laboratory.	and the Persian Gulf States), Central and Eastern Europe and the Former Soviet Union, and the Pacific Ocean Islands (except New Zealand and Australia). Candidates must hold a doctoral degree in the biomedical or behavioral sciences, earned within the last 10 years; have no previous pre—or postdoctoral research training in the U.S.; and have an invitation from a scientist at a U.S. nonprofit institution. Applicants resident in the U.S. at the time of application are not eligible.	search experience. Round-trip air travel is provided. The U.S. host institution receives an allowance to cover mandatory health insurance of the fellow only, trips to domestic scientific meetings, and incidental research expenses. There is no extra allowance for dependents.
Senior International Fellowship	The Senior International Fellowship (SIF) Program provides opportunities for mid—and senior-career level U.S. scientists to conduct bio-medical research studies at foreign institutions. The SIF is intended to enhance the exchange of ideas and information in the biomedical and behavioral sciences.	Candidates must be U.S. citizens or permanent U.S. residents, hold a doctoral degree in one of the biomedical or behavioral sciences, and have 5 or more years of research experience beyond the degree. They must hold a full-time appointment on the staff of a public or private nonprofit research, clinical, or educational institution and must be invited by a nonprofit foreign institution.	Fellowships are for 3 to 12 months, which may be divided into as many as 3 terms utilized over a 3-year period. Awards provide a stipend and foreign living allowance, which may not exceed a total of $39,000; a research allowance of up to $6,000 per year, prorated at $500 per month for each visiting period; and economy class round-trip travel between the U.S. and the foreign host institution.

Program	Summary	Eligibility	Scope of Support
Foreign-Funded Fellowships for U.S. Scientists Going Abroad	The FIC administers fellowship programs for U.S. scientists to conduct research in nine foreign countries, supported by the following foreign agencies or institutions: The Academy of Finland, the Alexander von Humboldt Foundation (Germany), the Health Research Board of Ireland, the Israeli Ministry of Health, the Japan Society of the Promotion of Science (JSPS), the Norwegian Research Council for Science and the Humanities, the Swedish Medical Research Council and the Taiwan Visiting Scientists Program. The applicant must identify a sponsor in the host country either through direct correspondence, or through correspondence on the applicant's behalf between a senior scientist in the United States and a colleague in the host country.	Applicants must be U.S. citizens or permanent U.S. residents; hold a doctorate in one of the clinical, behavioral, or biomedical sciences; and have recent professional experience appropriate to the proposed study. Requirements for each fellowship depend on particular program requirements.	Awards generally cover the payment of a stipend and round-trip air fare for fellows. Support for health and accident insurance, living allowances, family travel expenses and language training varies and depends on the specific fellowship that is sought. Duration of support ranges from 3 to 24 months.
NIH Visiting Program	Provides scientists from other nations an opportunity to conduct collaborative research at NIH.	Appointments or fellowships under the Visiting Program must be requested by a senior investigator in	Stipends or salary schedules are based on levels of experience. $25,000 to $38,000 for Visiting

Program	Summary	Eligibility	Scope of Support
	Candidates are invited to participate by senior NIH scientists, based on the research needs of the host laboratory. There are three categories of Visiting Program participants: Visiting Fellows, Visiting Associates and Visiting Scientists.	an NIH laboratory. Appointments are open to scientists at all career levels. as follows: • scientists with a doctoral degree or its equivalent in the health sciences and not more than 3 of relevant postdoctoral experience years are eligible for appointments as Visiting Fellows; • scientists with 3 to 6 years of post-doctoral research experience are eligible for appointments as Visiting Associates; and • scientists with 6 or more years of post-doctoral research experience are eligible for appointments as Visiting Scientists.	Fellows $29,000 to $54,000 for Visiting Associates $42,000 to $89,000 for Visiting Scientists
Summer Institute in Japan	The FIC and the National Science Foundation jointly sponsor the Summer Institute in Japan Program. The program provides opportunities for U.S. doctoral candidates to gain exposure to the Japanese research environment and culture, with the expectation that associations will be established that assist later scientific collaboration.	U.S. students pursuing a doctoral degree in the biomedical and behavioral sciences.	Awards provide for internships of approximately 8 weeks during the ummer months within a Japanese government, corporate or university laboratory; intensive language training in Japan; and curricula on U.S.-Japan comparative science policy, Japanese science, culture, history and political institutions. NIH supports

Program	Summary	Eligibility	Scope of Support
			travel costs to and from Japan and an allowance of $2,000 to each participant; the Japanese government provides dormitory accommodations as well as food and professional travel allowances.

Source: NIH 1996. *Research Training and Career Development Programs Supported by the National Institute of Health.* Bethesda, August, pp. 118–123

Appendix C

Types of Visas in Use at NIH

ECFMG J-1 (Alien Physician): Under the NIH's Exchange Visitor Program (J-I visa - Research Scholar category), any clinical responsibilities are limited to incidental patient contact, and credit for medical specialty board certification is not available. To have full patient contact, and credit for medical specialty board certification, foreign scientists at NIH must conduct their research under a J-1 visa sponsored by the Educational Commission for Foreign Medical Graduates (ECFMG) in those programs at NIH that meet graduate medical education or training accreditation standards.

NIH J-1 (Research Scholar): A Research Scholar is an individual primarily conducting research, observing, or consulting in connection with a research project at research institutions, corporate research facilities, museums, libraries, post-secondary accredited institutions, or similar types of institutions. The research scholar may also teach or lecture, unless disallowed by the sponsor. Regulations state that "a primary purpose of the Exchange Visitor Program is to foster the exchange of ideas between Americans and foreign nationals and to stimulate international collaborative teaching and research efforts. The exchange of professors and research scholars promotes interchange; mutual enrichment, and linkages between research and educational institutions in the United States and foreign countries."

J-2: (Dependents of Exchange Visitors): The spouse and unmarried minor children of a J-I exchange visitor who accompany or follow to join the principal participant in the United States are usually admitted in the J-2 classification, but they are not exchange visitors . . . Participants are not permitted to bring dependents to the United States in J-2 classification if adequate funding for their support and health insurance coverage is not available. Dependents who . . . accompany the principal exchange visitor to the United States obtain their J-2 visas and enter the United States in J-2 status along with the J-1 exchange visitor . . . J-2 dependents may apply to the district office of INS having jurisdiction over their place of temporary residence for permission to accept employment, provided the income from such employment will be "used to support the family's customary recreational and cultural activities and related travel, among other things. Employment will not be authorized if this income is needed to support the J-1 principal alien."

H-1B: An H-1B temporary worker is defined as a person who will perform services in a specialty occupation. Formerly, the nonimmigrant H-1B classification was available to aliens of 'distinguished merit and ability' or professionals. As of October 1991, the H-1B classification is available for those occupations that require 'theoretical and practical application of a body of highly specialized knowledge and attainment of a bachelor's or higher degree in the specific specialty or its equivalent as a minimum entry into the occupation in the United States . . . The regulations implementing the Act further define specialty occupations to include such fields as architecture, engineering, mathematics, physical sciences, social sciences, medicine and health education, business specialties, accounting, law, theology, and the arts.

O-1: Aliens of extraordinary ability in the sciences, arts, education, and athletics, plus aliens of extraordinary achievement in the motion picture and television industries . . . Extraordinary ability must have been demonstrated through sustained national or international acclaim . . . O visas are valid for up to three years, with 1-year incremental extensions allowed to continue the same work. The total time allowed to stay in the United States is the duration of the 'event' (event means an activity such as, but not limited to, a scientific project, conference, convention, lecture series, tour, exhibit, academic year or other engagement). Such activity could include short vacations, promotional appearances, and stopovers incidental or related to the event. A group of related activities will also be considered an event for which the visa is granted. Thus there is no absolute limit an O-1 can stay in the United States. The O category applies to individuals, not groups. A successful petition for O status must establish the fact that the applicant has demonstrated extraordinary ability and must include a written consultation from a peer group (means a group or organization composed of and governed by practitioners of the alien's occupation who are of similar standing with the alien) in the area of the alien's expertise. O visa status requires considerable documentation and appears to be best reserved for the most highly qualified guest professors, researchers, and artists. Extraordinary ability in the sciences, education, or business means a level of expertise indicating that the individual is one of the small percentage who have risen to the very top of their field of endeavor.

F-1: An F-1 visa may be granted to an alien "who is a bona fide student qualified to pursue a full course of study" at an academic or language institution authorized to admit foreign students. Students who have completed requirements for a doctorate may be offered the opportunity for advanced study at the postdoctoral level. Under certain conditions such students are eligible to apply for F-1 visas to come to the United States, to continue in F-1 status for the new educational program at the school they were last authorized to attend, to effect a transfer in F-1 status to begin a new educational program, or to change nonimmigrant classification in order to undertake postdoctoral study. Although no time limit for postdoctoral study is set by regulation, INS has directed its officers to look into cases where it appears that the student may engage in postdoctoral study for more than 3 years. Deviations from the full-course-of study requirement include postdoctoral students or fellows. These are not enrolled for student registration credit and therefore may not appear on course-enrollment lists. They are considered to be pursuing full courses of study, however, if they are carrying on the research and studies for which they were issued the [required permit].

B-1 (visitors for business): According to federal regulations, the term 'business' [for purposes of defining a B-1 visitor] refers to "legitimate activities of a commercial or professional character. It does not include purely local employment or labor for hire . . . An alien of distinguished merit and ability seeking to enter the United States temporarily with the idea of performing temporary services of an exceptional nature, requiring merit and ability, but having no contract or other prearranged employment, may be classified as a . . . visitor for business . . . The Department of State has elaborated upon the types of people who can be issued B-I visas:

- Aliens coming to engage in commercial transactions that do not involve gainful employment in the United States, to participate in scientific, educational, professional, or business conventions or conferences, or to undertake independent research;
- An alien already employed abroad coming to undertake training who would be classifiable as H-3, but who will continue to receive a salary from the foreign employer and will receive no salary or other remuneration from a U.S. source other than an expense allowance or other reimbursement for expenses incidental to temporary stay.

B-1 visitors cannot legally accept full-time, part-time, or temporary teaching or research positions or other employment for which they are paid by a U.S. institution. B-1 visitors who accept such positions violate the terms of their status and become subject to deportation. However, it is legal for an educational institution to pay a subsistence allowance to a B-1 visitor who performs a temporary service, to reimburse expenses, or to pay an honorarium that does not exceed travel and living costs. B-1 visitors may be admitted to the United States for an initial period of no longer than 1 year and may be granted extensions of stay in increments no longer than 6 months each.

TN: Canadian and Mexican aliens entering as professionals under the North America Free Trade Agreement.

G-4: Officers, or employees of international organizations, and the members of their immediate families.

EAD: Employment Authorization Document – The document issued to certain aliens allowed to work in the United States under several types of visas for specific employers.

A-1/A-2: An A-1 alien is defined as "an ambassador, public minister, or career diplomatic or consular officer who has been accredited by a foreign government . . . and the members of the alien's immediate family. A-I aliens are admired for the duration of their status in this classification. A foreign government official in A-1 status may be employed only by the foreign government entity. Members of the immediate family residing with an A-1 diplomat may apply for employment permission. The regulations prescribe strict limitations on the approval of such employment.

A-2 aliens are defined as "other officials and employees who have been accredited by a foreign government . . . and the members of their immediate families." Family members may apply for employment permission under the same terms as those described above for A-1 family members. A-1 and A-2 visa holders may attend school full or part time while maintaining their status.

Sources: NAFSA: *Advisor's Manual of Federal Regulations Affecting Foreign Students and Scholars.* Washington, DC. Association of International Educators. Alex Bedrosian, Editor. 1993.

Appendix D

Trends in the Number of Foreign Scientists at NIH by Country of Origin, 1970, 1980, 1990, 1996, and 1998

Country	1970	1980	1990	1996	1998
Afghanistan	1				
Albania				1	1
Algeria		2	1	1	2
Argentina	4	9	43	31	27
Armenia				1	1
Australia	12	23	33	32	42
Austria		9	10	8	9
Bahamas			1		
Bangladesh	2	2	5		
Belarus	2	4			
Belgium	2	16	9	13	9
Bermuda	1				
Bosnia-Hercegovina	2	2			
Brazil	10	31	27	30	
Bulgaria	1	4	8	10	
Burkina Faso	1	1			
Cameroon	1	1			
Canada	4	41	52	93	135
Chile	4	3	15	9	8
China, People's Republic	2	10	188	269	326
Colombia	1	5	2	5	
Congo	1	1			
Costa Rica	1				
Croatia	6	6			
Cuba	1				

Country	1970	1980	1990	1996	1998
Cyprus	2	1	2		
Czech Republic	16				
Czechoslovakia & Slovak Federation	5	3	17	13	
Denmark	1	3	7	12	11
Egypt	8	2	1	2	
El Salvador	1				
Estonia	2	2			
Ethiopia	1	3	3		
Fiji	1				
Finland	12	13	14	22	
France	2	27	63	75	90
Georgia	2	1			
Germany	13	18	63	132	119
Ghana	3	1			
Greece	14	18	19	17	
Guyana	1	2			
Hong Kong	9	4	4		
Hungary	8	51	36	29	
Iceland	1	1	2	2	
India	9	114	103	104	126
Iran	1	4	3	8	7
Iraq	1	1	2		
Ireland	2	10	5	6	
Israel	12	71	77	49	52
Italy	14	71	139	149	132
Jamaica	1	2	1		
Japan	51	199	351	318	332
Jordan	1	2	2		
Kenya	1	1			
Korea	1	12	47	91	147
Latvia	1				
Lebanon	4	3	5	3	
Liberia	1				
Lithuania	1				
Luxembourg	3				
Malawi	1				
Malaysia	3	4	3		
Mali	1	2			
Malta	1				
Mexico	1	7	8	4	15
Mongolia	2	1			
Morocco	1	8	5		
Nepal	1	1			
Netherlands	1	9	28	37	34
New Zealand	1	3	9	14	8
Nigeria	4	3	3	3	
Norway	1	3	1	1	
Pakistan	2	4	5	9	11

Country	1970	1980	1990	1996	1998
Peru	3	1	4	3	
Philippines	2	6	11	8	8
Poland	16	39	32	35	
Portugal	2	3	5		
Romania	1	1	3	4	
Russia				119	108
Saudi Arabia	1				
Senegal	1				
Serbia	8	4			
Sierra Leone	2	1	1		
Singapore	3	3	4		
Slovak Republic	16	19			
Slovenia	1				
South Africa	1	3	6	9	4
Spain	2	10	36	54	53
Sri Lanka	3	1	3	3	
Stateless	10	2			
Sudan	1	1			
Swaziland	1	1			
Sweden	2	32	7	12	11
Switzerland	2	19	26	17	14
Syria	1				
Taiwan	7	23	17	24	23
Tanzania	1				
Thailand	1	2	6	8	
Trinidad and Tobago	2	1			
Tunisia	1	2	1		
Turkey	5	5	11	16	
Ukraine	9	10			
United Kingdom	24	82	109	84	106
United States	11	21	4	7	2
Uruguay	1	1	1		
USSR			20		
Uzbekistan	1	1			
Venezuela	2	5	5	3	
Vietnam	1	1	3	3	
Yugoslavia	2	18	1		
Zaire	1	1			
Zimbabwe	1	1			
Total	199	985	1756	2097	2295

Source: NIH unpublished data.

Appendix E

New Intramural
Professional Designations

	Characteristics			Appointment Mechanism Options				Title 42 Service Fellow		Non FTE Fellow			Unpaid by NIH	
Intramural Professional Designation	Tenured	Permanent	Independent (requires BSC review)	General Schedule (GS)	Commissioned Corps (CC)	SES (SSS)	SBRS	U.S. or Permanent Resident	Visiting Program VA/VS	IRTA**	Visiting Fellow	IPA or Expert	Guest Researcher	Special Volunteer
Senior Investigator	Yes	Yes	Yes	Yes	Yes	Yes	Yes	Possibly***	Yes					
Investigator (Tenure-Track)	No	No	Yes		(Limited Tour)		Rarely	Yes	Yes					
Staff Scientist/ Staff Clinician	No	Possibly, by Exception	No	By Exception	By Exception			Yes	Yes					
Research Fellow/ Clinical Fellow (<8 years)	No	No	No		(Limited Tour)			Yes	Yes			Yes		
Postdoctoral Fellow (<5 years)	No	No	No							Yes	Yes		Yes	Yes
Senior Research Assistant (GS-12 & above)/ Research Assistant (GS-11 & below)	No	Yes	No	Yes										
Adjunct Investigator*	No	Possibly, if in a Non-IRP component	Possibly	Yes	Yes	Yes		Yes	Yes			Yes	Yes	Yes
Student (High School through Graduate/Medical School)	No	No	No	Yes						Yes	Yes		Yes	Yes

Note: A foreign scientist approved by the DDIR for designation as Senior Investigator, Investigator, or Staff Scientist/Staff Clinician will be supported for J-1 visa waiver/permanent resident status (green card) if this is necessary.

* Adjunct investigator refers to an individual working full or part-time in an intramural setting, whose primary career appointment is elsewhere (e.g., extramural NIH program, medical school or university faculty on sabbatical), often but not always on non-NIH support, and usually more than 8-years postdoctoral.

** Includes NRSA, NCI Biotech Fellows, etc.

*** For retiring Commissioned officers and decertified SBRS members.

References

Bhagwati, Jagdish and Milind Rao. 1996. "Foreign Students in Science and Engineering Ph.D. Programs: An Alien Invasion or Brain Drain?" In B. Lindsay Lowell, editor. *Temporary Migrants in the United States*. U.S. Commission on Immigration Reform. Washington, DC, pp. 265–287.

Caskey, C. Thomas. 1996. "The Future of Biotechnology." In Frederick B. Rudolph and Larry V. McIntire, editors."*Biotechnology: Science, Engineering, and Ethical Challenges for the 21ᵗ.Century*. National Academy of Sciences: Joseph Henry Press. Washington, DC, pp. 43–59.

Chen, Jr., Philip S. 1992. "The National Institutes of Health and Its Interactions with Industry." In Roger J. Porter and Thomas E. Malone, editors. *Biomedical Research: Collaboration and Conflict of Interest*. The Johns Hopkins University Press. Baltimore, MD, pp. 199–221.

Chiswick, Barry R. 1996. "Policy Analysis of Foreign Student Visa." In B. Lindsay Lowell, editor. *Temporary Migrants in the United States*. U.S. Commission on Immigration Reform. Washington, DC, pp. 233–245.

Clutter, Mary. 1996. Statement submitted to the Hearing on Computational Biology. Subcommittee on Science, Technology and Space Committee on Commerce, Science, and Transportation. U.S. Senate, September 17.

DeFreitas, Gregory. 1996. "Nonimmigrant Visa Programs: Problems and Policy Reforms." In B. Lindsay Lowell, editor. *Temporary Migrants in the United States*. U.S. Commission on Immigration Reform. Washington, DC, pp. 189–198.

Dibner, Mark D. 1997. *Biotechnology Guide U.S.A. – Companies, Data and Analysis* (fourth edition). Institute for Biotechnology Information. Research Triangle Park, North Carolina.

Dustira, Alicia K. 1992. "The Funding of Basic and Clinical Biomedical Research." In Roger J. Porter and Thomas E. Malone, editors. *Biomedical Research: Collaboration and Conflict of Interest*. The Johns Hopkins University Press. Baltimore, MD, pp. 33–56.

Eisenberg, Rebecca.1996. "Patents: Help or Hindrance to Technology Transfer?" In Frederick B. Rudolph and Larry V. McIntire, editors."*Biotechnology: Science, Engineering, and Ethical Challenges for the 21ᵗ.Century*. National Academy of Sciences: Joseph Henry Press. Washington, DC, pp. 161–172.

Ellis, R.A. 1994. "At the Crossroads: Crisis and Opportunity for American Engineers in the 1990s." *Engineering Workforce Bulletin* (special edition), Numbers130–131.

Espenshade, Thomas J. and German Rodriguez. 1996. "Completing the Ph.D.: Comparative Performance of U.S. and Foreign Students.""*Social Science Quarterly*, 78:2, pp. 593–605.

Finn, Michael G., Leigh Ann Pennington, and Kathryn Hart Anderson. 1995. "Foreign Nationals Who Receive Science and Engineering Ph.D.s from U.S. Universities." Oak Ridge Institute for Science and Education.

Hagan, Jacqueline and Susana McCollom. 1996. "Skill Level and Employer Use of Foreign Specialty Worker." In B. Lindsay Lowell, editor. *Temporary Migrants in the United States*. U.S. Commission on Immigration Reform. Washington, DC, pp. 163–187.

Hoxby, Caroline M. 1998. "Do Immigrants Crowd Disadvantaged American Natives Out of Higher Education?" In Daniel S. Hamermesh and Frank D. Bean, editors, *Help or Hindrance? The Economic Implications of Immigration for African Americans*. Russell Sage Foundation: New York, pp. 282–321.

Keely, Charles B. 1996. "Visa Policy of the United States." In B. Lindsay Lowell, editor. *Temporary Migrants in the United States*. U.S. Commission on Immigration Reform. Washington, DC, pp. 103–125.

Keely, Charles B. 1997. "Recruitment of Foreign High level Human Resources: Employer Behavior and Perspectives." Discussion paper presented at the Workshop on the Migration of Scientists and Engineers to the United States. Institute for Economic Development: Boston University.

Kolberg, Rebecca. 1996. "Land of Milk and Honey? NIH Through the Eyes of Foreign Scientists." *The NIH Catalyst.* Vol.4, Issue 1, pp. 1, 10–12.

Kramer, Roger G. 1999. "Developments in International Migration to the United States: 1998." U.S. Department of Labor, Bureau of International Labor Affairs, Immigration Policy and Research: Washington, DC. Working Paper 33.

Lowell, B. Lindsay. 1996. "Temporary Visas for Work, Study, and Cultural Exchange: Introduction and Summary." In B. Lindsay Lowell, editor. *Temporary Migrants in the United States*. U.S. Commission on Immigration Reform. Washington, DC, pp. 1–28.

Lowell, B. Lindsay, editor. 1996. *Temporary Migrants in the United States*. U.S. Commission on Immigration Reform. Washington, DC.

Malone, Thomas E. 1992. "The Moral Imperative for Biomedical Research." In Roger J. Porter and Thomas E. Malone, editors. *Biomedical Research: Collaboration and Conflict of Interest*. The Johns Hopkins University Press. Baltimore, MD, pp. 3–32.

Matloff, Norman. 1993. "Presentation to the California State Assembly Select Committee on Immigration."

Matloff, Norman. 1997. "The Role of Immigration in Computer Fields: A Critical Analysis." Discussion paper presented at the Workshop on the Migration of Scientists and Engineers to the United States. Institute for Economic Development: Boston University.

McKelvey, Maureen D. 1996."*Evolutionary Innovations: The Business of Biotechnology*. Oxford University Press. Oxford.

Morris, Sr., Frank L. 1996. "Denial of Doctoral Opportunities for African Americans." In B. Lindsay Lowell, editor."*Temporary Migrants in the United States*. U.S. Commission on Immigration Reform. Washington, DC, pp. 247–264.

National Institutes of Health. 1994. Report of the External Advisory Committee of the Director's Advisory Committee. Intramural Program. Bethesda, MD.

National Research Council. 1992. *U.S.-Japan Technology Linkages in Biotechnology: Challenges for the 1990s*. National Academy Press. Washington, DC.

National Research Council. 1998. *Trends in the Early Careers of Life Scientists*. National Academy Press. Washington, DC.

National Science Foundation. 1995. "Impact of Emerging Technologies on the Biological Sciences: Report of a Workshop." June 26–27. www.nsf.gov/bio/pubs/stctechn/stcmain.htm.

North, David S. 1995. *Soothing the Establishment*. University Press of America. Lanham, MD.

North, David S. 1996. "Some Thoughts on Nonimmigrant Student and Workers Program." In B. Lindsay Lowell, editor. *Temporary Migrants in the United States*. U.S. Commission on Immigration Reform. Washington, DC, pp. 61–102.

O'Connell, William. 1991. "Foreign Students in the United States: The Orphans of International Education." Institute for Higher Education, Law and Governance. IHELG Monograph 91–1. Houston, TX: University of Houston Law Center.

"On Cabbages and Kings: The IUBMB "Problems and Prospects." 1997. *Trends in Biochemical Sciences*, 22, August, p. 281.

Papademetriou, Demetrios G. and Stephen Yale-Loehr. 1995. *Putting the National Interest First: Rethinking the Selection of Skilled Immigrants*. Executive Summary. International Migration Policy Program: Carnegie Endowment for International Peace.

Papademetriou, Demetrios G. 1996. "Skilled Temporary Workers in the Global Economy: Creating a Balanced and Forward-Looking Selection Process." In B. Lindsay Lowell, editor. *Temporary Migrants in the United States*. U.S. Commission on Immigration Reform. Washington, DC, pp. 29–60.

Parkin, Gene F.1996 "Bioremediation: A Promising Technology." In Frederick B. Rudolph and Larry V. McIntire, editors."*Biotechnology: Science, Engineering, and Ethical Challenges for the 21ˢᵗ Century*. National Academy of Sciences: Joseph Henry Press. Washington, DC, pp. 113–130.

Perkins, John P. 1996. "Are U.S. Universities Producing Too Many Ph.D.'s in the Biomedical Sciences: Facts and Artifacts." *Pharmacology '96 John V. Croker Memorial Lecture*. American Society for Pharmacology and Experimental Therapeutics. Bethesda, MD.

Rao, Milind. 1993. "Migration of Talent: Foreign Students and Graduate Economics in the U.S." Working Papers. The Jerome Levy Economics Institute. Bard College, Annandale-on-Hudson, NY.

Regets, Mark C. 1995. "Preparing the U.S. Scientist for the 21ˢᵗ Century: A Plan for Graduate Education and Postdoctoral Training for the Mathematical and Physical Sciences." Background paper for the NSF Mathematical and Physical Sciences Directorate Workshop. National Science Foundation. Washington, DC.

"Research Job Shortage May Broaden Scope of Training Programs." 1995. *Journal of NIH Research*. Vol. 7. January, pp. 32–33.

Rhein, Reginald. 1990. "After the Wall: East-West Scientific Exchanges Escalate." *Journal of NIH Research*, pp. 73–76.

Roberts, Dhauna S. 1991. "NIH's Intramural Research Program: The Once and Future King?" *Journal of NIH Research.* Vol. 3, pp. 20–26.

Schultz, Jerome. 1996. "Interactions Between Universities and Industries." In Frederick B. Rudolph and Larry V. McIntire, editors."*Biotechnology: Science, Engineering, and Ethical Challenges for the 21ˢᵗ Century.* National Academy of Sciences: Joseph Henry Press. Washington, D.C., pp. 131–146.

Schultz, T. Paul. 1995. *Immigrant Quality and Assimilation: A Review of the Literature.* Research Papers. U.S. Commission on Immigration Reform. Washington, DC.

Shuler, Michael.1996. "Development of Biopharmaceuticals: An Engineering Perspective." In Frederick B. Rudolph and Larry V. McIntire, editors."*Biotechnology: Science, Engineering, and Ethical Challenges for the 21ˢᵗ Century.* National Academy of Sciences: Joseph Henry Press. Washington, DC, pp. 100–112.

Smith, Michael P. 1996. "The New High-Tech Braceros? Who is the Employer? What is the Problem?" In B. Lindsay Lowell, Editor. *Temporary Migrants in the United States.* U.S. Commission on Immigration Reform. Washington, DC, pp. 127–161.

Sowers, Arthur E. 1997. "Contemporary Problems in Science Jobs." www.access. digex.net/ arthures/homepage.htm, p.2.

Tomlinson, Eric.1996. "Effect of the New Biologies on Health Care." In Frederick B. Rudolph and Larry V. McIntire, editors."*Biotechnology: Science, Engineering, and Ethical Challenges for the 21ˢᵗ Century.* National Academy of Sciences: Joseph Henry Press. Washington, DC, pp. 63–71.

U.S. Commission on Immigration Reform. 1994. *U.S. Immigration Policy: Restoring Credibility.* Washington, DC.

U.S. Commission on Immigration Reform. 1995. *Legal Immigration: Setting Priorities: A Report to Congress.* Washington, DC.

U.S. Congress: Office of Technology Assessment. 1991. *Biotechnology in a Global Economy.* OTA-BA–494. U.S. Government Printing Office, Washington, DC.

U.S. Department of Labor. 1996. *The Department of Labor's Foreign Labor Certification Programs: The System Is Broken and Needs to be Fixed.* Washington, DC: Office of Inspector General.

U.S. General Accounting Office. 1996. *Foreign Physicians: Exchange Visitor Program Becoming Major Route to Practicing in U.S. Underserved Areas.* Washington, DC.

Valbrun, Marjorie. 1999. "Fraud Concerns Grow Over Employment-Visa Program." *The Wall Street Journal.* July 12: A30.

Vaughan, Christopher C., Bruce L. R. Smith, and Roger J. Porter. 1992. "The Contribution of Biomedical Science and Technology to U.S. Economic Competitiveness." In Roger J. Porter and Thomas E. Malone, editors. *Biomedical Research: Collaboration and Conflict of Interest.* The Johns Hopkins University Press. Baltimore, MD, pp. 57–76.

Zacher, Robert. 1997. "Remarks made at the Workshop on the Migration of Scientists and Engineers to the United States." Institute for Economic Development, Boston University. Boston. May 21.

Index

AIDS International Training and Research Program (AITRP). *See* Fogarty International Center (FIC)

American Red Cross, 35

American Society for Human Genetics, 35

American Society for Pharmacology and Experimental Therapeutics, 35

Bayer Corporation, 133

Bayh-Dole Act. *See* Patent and Trademark Laws Amendment (1980)

Biomedical association perspective
  foreign students
    NIH opportunities, 128
    postdoctoral employment, 127–28
    temporary vs. permanent status, 129
    training, 127–28, 129
    university opportunities, 127–28
    work ethics, 129
  government funding, 128
  immigration policy implications, 126, 127
    taxation, 127
  international competition implications, 128
  labor demand cycles, 126–27
  labor force impact, 126–27
    political role, 126–27
  labor policy implications, 128–29
  overview, 113
  study objectives, 125–26
  summary, 130
  U.S. students
    specialization shortage, 126

    training, 126, 127–28

Biomedical employment impact
  administrator perspective
    current, 81–83
    former, 83
  adverse implications, 81, 82, 83–84, 85, 86–87, 89–90
  beneficial implications, 81, 82–83, 85, 86–87, 88–89
  biotechnology industry trends, 22–24, 86–87
  doctoral education, 24–31
    completion time, 26
    elite university recruitment, 26, 27–28
    employment settings, 25–26
    employment time, 25–26
    foreign/American scientist contrast, 28–31
    foreign/American trainee contrast, 28–31, 40
    oversupply, 81, 84, 85, 86
    recommendations for, 30–31
    tenure, 27–28, 88, 89
  foreign scientist availability, 83, 84, 87
  foreign trainee perspective
    current, 87–88
    former, 88–90
  funding limitations, 81, 84
  globalization role, 11–17, 22–24, 86, 87
  knowledge internationalization, 86
  labor demand cycles, 81, 84, 86, 87, 88, 89–90
  language proficiency, 83, 87

For Product Safety Concerns and Information please contact our EU
representative GPSR@taylorandfrancis.com
Taylor & Francis Verlag GmbH, Kaufingerstraße 24, 80331 München, Germany

www.ingramcontent.com/pod-product-compliance
Lightning Source LLC
Chambersburg PA
CBHW050436280326
41932CB00013BA/2144